CORRUPTING the WORD of GOD

THE HISTORY *of the* WELL-MEANT OFFER

Herman Hanko
Mark H. Hoeksema

REFORMED
FREE PUBLISHING
ASSOCIATION
Jenison, Michigan

Scripture cited is taken from the King James (Authorized) Version

Reformed Free Publishing Association
1894 Georgetown Center Drive
Jenison, Michigan 49428
616-457-5970
rfpa.org
mail@rfpa.org

Cover design by Erika Kiel
Interior design and typesetting by Katherine Lloyd, The DESK

ISBN 978-1-944555-10-8
Ebook 978-1-944555-11-5
LCCN 2016952842

Dedicated to the faithful ministers, all now in heaven, who fought through the difficult years of 1924 to 1954 to maintain the heritage and truth established in the Protestant Reformed Churches: Cornelius Hanko, John Heys, Homer Hoeksema, Henry Kuiper, George Lubbers, Marinus Schipper, Herman Veldman, and Gerrit Vos

CONTENTS

We are not as many, which corrupt the word of God: but as of sincerity, but as of God, in the sight of God speak we in Christ.—*2 Corinthians 2:17*

For I am not ashamed of the gospel of Christ: for it is the power of God unto salvation to every one that believeth; to the Jew first, and also to the Greek. For therein is the righteousness of God revealed from faith to faith: as it is written, The just shall live by faith.—*Romans 1:16–17*

Preface

⟺

Most of the content of this book was originally developed and presented by Prof. Herman Hanko for an interim course in the Theological School of the Protestant Reformed Churches.

Recently it has become evident from literature published by Reformed and Presbyterian writers that there is renewed interest in the subject of the well-meant offer of the gospel, and this teaching is the subject of wide discussion and controversy. The Reformed Free Publishing Association is pleased to present this contribution to the debate from the viewpoint of its history.

The original material has been edited and in some instances rewritten and expanded, primarily by Professor Hanko. The core ideas, however, remain unchanged. They clearly set forth the history of the corruption of the word of God called the well-meant offer.

Of note is that Professor Hanko is the author of the first ten chapters and chapters 13 and 14. Chapters 11 and 12, written by Mark H. Hoeksema, are profitably added to the history presented in this book.

Rev. Angus Stewart provides a selected annotated bibliography for additional interest in and research of the subject of this book.

May this study of the history of the well-meant offer of the gospel be a blessing to God's people, who resist this corruption of the word of God and find the gospel to be not an offer but the power of God unto salvation.

—Mark H. Hoeksema

INTRODUCTION

⟨⟩

While the doctrine of common grace was a central issue in the controversies that led to the establishment of the Protestant Reformed Churches, imbedded in the formulation of the doctrine of common grace was the almost hidden doctrine of the well-meant offer of the gospel. It is part of the first of three doctrinal statements formulated and adopted by the Christian Reformed Church at its synod in 1924.

> Concerning the first point, with regard to the favorable disposition of God toward mankind in general, and not only to the elect, Synod declares that according to the Scripture and the confessions it is determined that besides the saving grace of God, shown only to the elect unto eternal life, there is a certain kind of favor or grace of God which He shows to His creatures in general. This is evidenced by the quoted Scripture passages and from the Canons of Dort 2.5 and 3–4.8–9, which deals with the general offer of the Gospel; whereas the quoted declarations of Reformed writers from the golden age of Reformed theology also give evidence that our Reformed fathers from of old have advocated these opinions.[1]

---

1   *1924 Acts of Synod of the Christian Reformed Church Held from 18 June until 8 July 1924 in Kalamazoo, MI, USA*, trans. Henry De Mots (Grand Rapids, MI: Calvin College, Archives of the Christian Reformed Church), 145–46.

In the discussions that followed the adoption of that statement of doctrine, the reference to the well-meant offer was often called the main point of the first point. While my intention in this book is to deal specifically with the doctrine of the well-meant offer of the gospel, my point is that a denial of the well-meant offer is an important reason for the existence of the Protestant Reformed Churches as a denomination. The three points of common grace as a whole and the main point of the first point, in spite of any claim to the contrary, have never been the teaching of the church of Christ.

The denial of the well-meant offer of the gospel by the Protestant Reformed Churches has set them apart from almost every ecclesiastical fellowship. Today it is difficult to find a Reformed or Presbyterian denomination that is not officially or unofficially committed to the well-meant offer. Not only is the well-meant offer widely accepted, but also the charge of hyper-Calvinism is hurled against those who deny it. The idea behind the charge is that true Calvinism includes the well-meant offer of the gospel. It is alleged that those who repudiate the well-meant offer are not faithful to the teachings of Calvin or to the genius of Calvinism.

My purpose is to trace the history of the idea of the well-meant offer throughout the history of the church of the new dispensation. Where did the idea originate? How did it creep into the church? What is its place in the historical development of the truth throughout the ages? Who taught it and who did not? Has the church of Christ, guided by the Spirit of truth, consistently and repeatedly repudiated it? Standing without proof is the bold statement of the authors of common grace that "Reformed writers from the golden age of Reformed theology also give evidence that our Reformed fathers from of old have advocated these opinions."[2] Can this claim be proved? Or is it an empty claim used to defend a position that has no real proof?

I am not arguing in this historical overview that the faith of the church of the past is in any way decisive in determining the truth or falsity of the doctrine of a well-meant offer. Scripture alone is the rule of faith and life. Regardless of what the church in former years may or may not have taught, the history of that doctrine may not determine whether we should accept it or repudiate it.

Yet a study of how the church in the past dealt with this doctrine is important. The authors of common grace appeal not only to scripture and the confessions, but also to theologians from the "golden age of Reformed theology" in support of their position. Is their claim true?

The question is also important because Christ promised his church that he would send them the Spirit of truth, who would guide the church into the truth (John 14:16–17, 26; 15:26; 16:7–13). While it is possible for the church to err in its official decisions on matters of the truth, historical testimony carries some weight, whether it is the united testimony of Reformed writers in the golden age of Reformed theology or, better yet, the testimony of the church for two millennia. Any individual or ecclesiastical body that claims a doctrine to be true that has been repeatedly declared by the church to be false not only must have studied thoroughly the history that he contradicts, but also must have studied all the relevant biblical and confessional testimony. One wonders whether there is not a certain arrogance when an individual or a church body claims to know better than the whole church since Pentecost.

---

2   Ibid., 146.

This cuts both ways. If a doctrine has not been taught and has been consistently and repeatedly repudiated, it is theologically dangerous to hold it as biblical. The one who does this is swimming in treacherous waters and is almost certain to drown.

The term *well-meant offer of the gospel* is of fairly recent vintage. The church prior to the Reformation of the sixteenth century did not use the term or any similar term. However, similar ideas and other doctrines associated with the well-meant offer have been discussed and debated by the church from the time of Augustine (d. 430). Augustine and his followers explained the same biblical texts that are used today to prove the well-meant offer. In their exegesis of these texts they repudiated the present-day interpretations and interpreted them in full harmony with orthodox theology through the ages. Worse yet, the interpretations of texts given by today's supporters of the well-meant offer are the same as those given in the past by heretics who repudiated the truth.

My contention in this book is that the doctrine of a well-meant offer of the gospel has been taught by those who repudiated other truths of scripture and taught doctrines contrary to the Christian faith and inseparably connected to a well-meant offer. My contention is also that the line of the biblical, Reformed faith not only consistently and frequently repudiated the necessary corollary doctrines of a well-meant offer, but also repudiated the doctrine itself and by name.

In this book I choose to use the term *well-meant offer of the gospel,* because it is a well-known and accurate description of the error. There are other names for this error. Sometimes it is called *free offer of the gospel* or *gracious offer of the gospel.* All three terms refer to the same doctrine.

Well-meant offer emphasizes God's sincerity in offering salvation in the gospel to all who hear it. The gospel announces

God's love for all men and his will and intention to save all men. *Free offer of the gospel* emphasizes that the salvation God accomplished in Christ is freely given to all who are moved by God's love for all men to accept the promises offered to them. *Gracious offer of the gospel* emphasizes that God's grace is shown to all men by his desire to save them and that he gives to everyone who hears the gospel the grace to receive it. The last term is the most accurate description of what the defenders of the doctrine claim the gospel says and does.

The fundamental questions are, is the grace of almighty God given only to the elect, whom he has chosen to be his beloved people, or are all men the objects and recipients of that grace? Is grace common or particular?

May God use this book to convince many that the gospel is not an offer but is still the power of God unto salvation to those who believe (Rom. 1:16).

—Herman Hanko

Chapter 1

PELAGIANISM AND SEMI-PELAGIANISM

A lthough the term *well-meant offer* came into use only after the Reformation, and although the doctrine was not discussed until the post-Reformation history of the church, the issues involved in the doctrine were on the agenda of the church already at the beginning of the fifth century. Discussion and debate over those issues were part of the controversy between Augustine, bishop of Hippo, and the Pelagians and semi-Pelagians. Augustine was a strong defender of sovereign and particular grace and has received the name *Doctor Gratiae* (doctor of grace). The origin of the well-meant offer of the gospel is connected with Pelagianism and semi-Pelagianism.

The well-meant offer of the gospel was not itself an explicit point of controversy in the first four centuries of the existence of the new dispensational church. The church in the first four centuries was preoccupied with many and varied controversies concerning the doctrine of the Trinity and the person and natures of Christ. Until the time of Augustine of Hippo (354–430), the church had paid very little attention to questions concerning anthropology and soteriology. The doctrine of free will was generally held in the early church, perhaps as a reaction to Manichean fatalism. However, the church also held to the truth of salvation by grace alone. The two obviously contradictory doctrines were held simultaneously with little thought given to how they could be reconciled. The issue was not closely examined or extensively studied in the light of scripture.

Although a certain freewillism may have predominated then, Athanasius' defense of the divinity of Christ at the Council of Nicea in 325 was an example of the early church's commitment to salvation by grace alone. He maintained that Christ had to be "true God of true God," [1] because salvation was exclusively God's work that came through Christ. Therefore, Christ had to be God.

Already at the time of Augustine the church was committed to the idea of meritorious good works, an idea that finally prevailed in Roman Catholic thought and was not banished from the thinking of the church until the Protestant Reformation in the sixteenth century. The idea of meritorious good works is intimately connected with the idea of free will, for good works cannot merit unless man has the power to perform them. This idea undoubtedly made it impossible for Augustinianism to prevail in the Roman Catholic Church after Augustine's death. The church was confronted with the question of whether to adopt a pure Augustinianism, which would require it to abandon its commitment to meritorious good works, or to hold to meritorious good works and turn its back on Augustine's teachings. The church chose the latter.

Pelagius taught that the will is absolutely free. He said that even after the fall man's will possesses the same power for

---

1 Nicene Creed, in *The Confessions and the Church Order of the Protestant Reformed Churches* (Grandville, MI: Protestant Reformed Churches in America, 2005), 11.

good and evil that Adam's will possessed before the fall. Whenever man is confronted with the choice of good or evil, he has the capability to choose either good or evil. Pelagius said that man's ability to choose the good is somewhat weakened by sin, but Pelagius saw sin as only a habit that does not affect man's nature. While a habit may become ingrained in a man's life, his will is not essentially affected, and his power to choose the good remains intact and unimpaired.

Augustine carried on his polemic against that heresy. As a result of his work, Pelagianism was officially condemned by the church at the Council of Carthage in 416 and at the Council of Ephesus in 431, held one year after Augustine's death.

Prior to Augustine's death, opposition to his teachings on particular and sovereign grace arose in various parts of the church, especially in southern Gaul. In opposition to Pelagius, Augustine taught the absolute inability of the human will of fallen and natural man to choose the good. Mankind fell in Adam, said Augustine, and the result of the fall for the whole human race was that man completely lost the ability to do the good and to will the good. His salvation was therefore dependent on grace. While Pelagius also spoke of grace, he insisted that grace was little more than a help, a measure of divine assistance, and was not essential to salvation. Augustine taught the absolute necessity of God's grace in salvation.

Other doctrines were necessarily involved. When Augustine was asked regarding the determining factor in who receives the gift of grace and who does not, his answer was sovereign predestination according to which God sovereignly chose his elect from eternity. The doctrines of sovereign grace and predestination were the occasion for controversy. In opposition to Augustine's views, theological positions similar to those connected with the well-meant offer were proposed.

One of Augustine's opponents was Cassian (360–435), who correctly may be called a semi-Pelagian. He did not agree with the position of Pelagius that the will is absolutely free, but Cassian insisted on maintaining that the will is free to a certain extent. He said that sin as it entered the human race through the fall of Adam does not rob man of a free will but does weaken man's will so that it is difficult for man to choose the good. Therefore, man needs divine assistance.

Just as Augustine's teaching of the inability of the human will to choose the good led him to the doctrine of sovereign predestination via the truth of sovereign grace, so Cassian proceeded from the idea of free will to the doctrine of divine love that wills the salvation of everyone. The two ideas are connected. If salvation is ultimately dependent on the choice of man's will and not on the choice of God's sovereign predestination, it is obvious that God loves all men and seeks the salvation of all men. God's love, which is all-embracing, extends thus to all men. Whether or not a man is ultimately saved depends on his response to the overtures of God's love.

Cassian's views were followed by those of Prosper of Aquitaine (390–455). There has always been some question whether Prosper actually taught semi-Pelagian views. This doubt arises from his extensive correspondence with Augustine, which was the chief means by which Augustine learned of the semi-Pelagian teachings of various theologians in Gaul. It is difficult to ascertain from Prosper's correspondence whether he expressed his opinions or merely informed Augustine of what others were teaching and asked for more light on those views.

However, it seems almost certain that Prosper did not agree completely with Augustine and that especially toward the end of Prosper's life he agreed substantially with Cassian. It is even possible that Prosper was responsible in some respects for advancing

Cassian's views. Prosper probably introduced into the discussion the distinction in the will of God between one will that is universal and conditional and another will that is particular and unconditional. Desiring in some sense to maintain the sovereignty of God in grace and predestination, and yet committed to free will, Prosper spoke of a will of God that expresses his desire to save everyone and another will that is particular, limited to the elect, and realized in the work of sovereign grace. One will is conditional; the other will is unconditional.

That Prosper was semi-Pelagian in his views is also substantiated by the contention of many that he wrote the pamphlet *De Vocatione Omnium Gentium*,[2] which dealt particularly with grace as it related to the controversy. The author made a distinction between general grace and particular grace. He said that general grace is connected with general revelation, because general revelation reveals the general grace of God to all men. In addition, general grace that comes through God's revelation in creation is inwardly applied to the heart of every man, so that it becomes the origin of all religion in man. The general grace that everyone receives expresses God's will that all men be saved.[3]

---

2 *De Vocatione Omnium Gentium* [The call of all nations], in *The Works of the Fathers in Translation*, ed. Johannes Quasten and Joseph C. Plumpe, trans. Joseph De Letter (Westminster, MD: The Newman Press, 1952).

3 The ideas that particular grace is built on general grace and that general grace is connected with general revelation are not foreign to many theologians who in recent years have adopted the well-meant offer of the gospel. See Herman Bavinck, *Our Reasonable Faith: A Survey of Christian Doctrine*, trans. Henry Zylstra (Grand Rapids, MI: Wm. B. Eerdmans Publishing Company, 1956), 32–60. See William Masselink, *General Revelation and Common Grace: A Defense of the Historic Reformed Faith over against the Theology and Philosophy of the So-called "Reconstructionist" Movement* (Grand Rapids, MI: Wm. B. Eerdmans Publishing Company, 1953), 67–162, 187–262.

Particular grace is given only to some and is necessary to salvation.

Augustine died in 430, and his disciples continued the theological battle.

Another opponent of Augustine was Faustus of Mileve, ordained bishop of Hippo in 454. He spoke of general grace that precedes special grace and is essential to special grace. General grace, bestowed without distinction on all men, becomes the means whereby the free will of man is preserved along with a certain religious and moral sense. Only when a man, by free will and the use of general grace, chooses the good is special grace given to him, by which he is actually saved. Thus for Faustus special grace was built on general grace, and salvation was dependent on the will of man.

To reinforce the contention that the well-meant offer is theologically connected with Pelagianism and semi-Pelagianism, it is significant that in Augustine's day the semi-Pelagians quoted the same scriptural texts that are used today to defend a general and gracious offer of the gospel: Matthew 23:37, Romans 2:4, 1 Timothy 2:4, and 2 Peter 3:9. Many of the objections the semi-Pelagians raised against Augustine's position were identical to the objections brought in our time against the truth of sovereign grace and eternal predestination. Augustine often chided his opponents for their interpretations of scripture and for being content with arguments from human reason. Augustine insisted that those scriptural passages apply only to the elect. In defending that position from scripture, he became increasingly convinced of the biblical soundness of his position and of the wrongness of the positions taken by his opponents. He reaffirmed and reemphasized the truths of sovereign grace in the whole work of salvation and of eternal and sovereign predestination.

Augustine wrote the following about Matthew 23:37:

Our Lord says plainly, however, in the Gospel, when upbraiding the impious city: "How often would I have gathered thy children together, even as a hen gathereth her chickens under her wings, and ye would not!" as if the will of God had been overcome by the will of men, and when the weakest stood in the way with their want of will, the will of the strongest could not be carried out. And where is that omnipotence which hath done all that it pleased on earth and in heaven, if God willed to gather together the children of Jerusalem, and did not accomplish it? or rather, Jerusalem was not willing that her children should be gathered together? But even though she was unwilling, He gathered together as many of her children as He wished: for He does not will some things and do them, and will others and do them not; but "He hath done all that He pleased in heaven and in earth."[4]

Regarding the interpretation of 1 Timothy 2:4, Augustine wrote:

We are to understand by "all men," the human race in all its varieties of rank and circumstances,—kings, subjects; noble, plebeian, high, low, learned, and unlearned; the sound in body, the feeble, the clever, the dull, the foolish, the rich, the poor, and those of middling circumstances; males, females, infants, boys, youths; young, middle-aged, and old men; of every tongue, of every fashion, of all arts, of all professions, with all the innumerable differences of will and conscience, and whatever else

---

4   Augustine, *Enchiridion* 97, in *The Nicene and Post-Nicene Fathers of the Christian Church*, ed. Philip Schaff, trans. J. F. Shaw (Grand Rapids, MI: Wm. B. Eerdmans Publishing Company, 1988), 3:268.

there is that makes a distinction among men...We are not compelled to believe that the omnipotent God has willed anything to be done which was not done: for, setting aside all ambiguities, if "He hath done all that He pleased in heaven and in earth," as the psalmist sings of Him, He certainly did not will to do anything that He hath not done.[5]

Augustine had one supporter of note, Fulgentius, who was a bishop of North Africa and a strong supporter of Augustinianism fifty years after Augustine's death. Fulgentius also commented on 1 Timothy 2:4, a verse the semi-Pelagians constantly appealed to in attempts to support their contentions that Christ died for all men and desired to save all men.

Truly, by these *all persons* whom God *wills* to be saved (1 Tim. 2:4) are signified not the entire human race completely, but the entirety of all who are to be saved. And, likewise, they are called "all" because divine goodness saves all those from all humanity, that is, from every nation, condition, and age, from every language and every province.[6]

Fulgentius proceeded to prove his interpretation of 1 Timothy 2:4 by appealing to Acts 3:38–39, Romans 8:28, and Psalm 115:3. He then wrote, "It is evil for someone to say that the Omnipotent is not able to do something that he willed to do...

---

5   Ibid., 270–71.
6   Fulgentius, *Epistula* 17, 61, 63, 66, quoted in Francis X. Gumerlock, *Fulgentius of Ruspe on the Saving Will of God: The Development of a Sixth-Century African Bishop's Interpretation of I Timothy 2:4 During the Semi-Pelagian Controversy* (Lewiston, NY: Edwin Mellen Press, 2009), 4, 96, 98–99.

Those whom he (i.e., the Son) wills to be given life are those whom he wills to be saved."[7]

Again referring to 1 Timothy 2:4, Fulgentius wrote, "Therefore, they are called 'all' because they are gathered from all kinds of persons, from all nations, from all conditions, from all masters, from all servants, from all kings, from all soldiers, from all provinces, from all languages, from all ages, and from all classes. Thus *all* are saved whom God *wills to be saved*."[8]

Fulgentius commented on Matthew 23:37, another favorite text of those who hold to the well-meant offer:

Whence our Savior reproves the malevolence of the unbelieving city with these words: *Jerusalem, Jerusalem, you who kill the prophets and stone those sent to you; how many times I yearned to gather your children together as a hen gathers her young under her wings, but you were unwilling* (Matt. 23:37). Christ said this to show its evil will by which it tried in vain to resist the invincible divine will, when God's good will neither could be conquered by those whom it deserts nor could not be able to accomplish anything which it wanted. That Jerusalem, insofar as it attained to its will, did not wish its children to be gathered to the Savior, but still he gathered all whom he willed. In this it wanted to resist the omnipotent but was unable to because God who, as it is written, *Whatever the Lord pleases, he does* (Psalm 135:6), converts to himself whomever he wills by a free justification, coming beforehand with his gift of superabounding grace on those whom he could justly damn if he wished.[9]

---

7   Ibid., 66.

8   Ibid.

9   Fulgentius, *De remissione peccatorum* 2.2–3, quoted in ibid., 64.

Fulgentius also commented on 2 Peter 3:9:

He [God] does not want anyone to perish, namely of those whom *he foreknew and predestinated to be conformed to the image of his Son* (Rom. 8:29). No one of these perishes. *For who opposes his will* (Rom. 9:19)? These are visited freely by the mercy of God before the end of this present life; they are moved for their salvation with a contrite and humbled heart and all by divine gift are converted to penance to which they are divinely predestined by free grace, so that, converted, they many not perish, but have life eternal...Because he who has done all things he wanted wants this, what he wants he always does invincibly. And so that is fulfilled in them which the unchangeable and invincible will of almighty God has, whose will, just as it cannot be changed in its plans, so neither is his power stopped or hindered in its execution; because neither is anyone able justly to censure his justice, nor can anyone stand opposed to his mercy...Therefore, when the Apostle Peter says that God *is patient, not wishing that any should perish, but that all should come to repentance* (2 Peter 3:9), let us not so understand the word "all" as stated above, as if there is no one who will not do a fitting penance, but we must understand "all" here as those to whom God gives penance in such a way that he may also give them the gift of perseverance.[10]

A quotation from Caesarius of Arles (c. 470–542) regarding 1 Timothy 2:4 will suffice to demonstrate that ancient expositors could exegete scripture better than some modern theologians.

---

10 Ibid., 62–64.

Caesarius was bishop of Arles, France, for forty years and is generally considered to be the most outstanding theologian of his time. He wrote in somewhat angry language his opposition to the position of the semi-Pelagians.

> But lifting yourself up in the most proud tribunal of your heart, you presume to judge God, saying...How does it seem [right] to him to will that the dew of divine grace remain in one cloud, that is, in the people of the Jews, through so many thousands of years, and that all of the other areas, that is, the whole world, did not deserve to be watered through the mercy of God? Or why afterward this one cloud, that is, the people of the Jews, would remain dry without the grace of God, and the areas of all the Gentiles would receive the dew of divine mercy?[11]

After quoting many other passages that emphasize God's irresistible will, Caesarius repeatedly asked why his opponents believed that God's will can be resisted, if God wills to save them. He ended with the charge that those men accused God and spoke against the apostle Paul.

The interpretations of these texts by the modern-day defenders of the well-meant offer of the gospel are identical to the interpretations given by the semi-Pelagians in Augustine's day. The interpretation by Augustine and some of his followers has been accepted by the church of Christ since the Reformation. The others have been repudiated.

Augustine's views did not prevail in the church of his day. Although several churchmen condemned to some extent the views of the semi-Pelagians, none stood firmly for the doctrines

---

11 Caesarius of Arles, *De gratia*, quoted in ibid., 163.

of Augustine. This was perhaps because the church had already committed itself to some idea of free will in its determination to preserve the merit of good works.[12]

In 529 the Council of Orange spoke on the controversy between Augustinianism and semi-Pelagianism, but its decisions were at best a compromise. While this council condemned certain aspects of the teachings of the semi-Pelagians and affirmed certain doctrines of Augustine, it refused to adopt a pure Augustinianism. It affirmed the doctrine of original sin and the unconditional necessity of grace, but it left room for the idea of sin as an illness rather than a spiritual death, and it was silent on the key doctrines of the absolute inability of the will to choose for the good and sovereign, double predestination. It warned against the idea of predestination to evil, something Augustine did not teach. In effect, semi-Pelagianism won the day.

What conclusions can be drawn from this history?

The idea of the offer of the gospel *per se* was not discussed at that time. This is understandable, because the whole truth concerning the preaching of the gospel did not receive theological attention, and no scriptural bases of the doctrine were established. The relationship between the views of the semi-Pelagians and preaching was not faced.

Further, although Augustine had outlined his basic position in the Pelagian controversy, the semi-Pelagians' attacks forced him to define his views more sharply and to defend them more carefully. The attacks of the semi-Pelagians brought Augustine back to scripture to study the passages involved and to reevaluate his work in the light of the word of God.

---

12 For a detailed study, see Herman C. Hanko, "Double Predestination: Augustine, Synod of Orange, and Gotteschalk" (master's thesis, Calvin Theological Seminary, 1986).

It is a striking fact that in the history of the church and of its doctrine there were only a few periods in which the doctrines of sovereign grace and predestination were maintained. Augustine taught and maintained these doctrines over against Pelagius and the semi-Pelagians. Although semi-Pelagianism gained the upper hand, the result of Augustine's work is still a legacy to the church today.

Several ideas that throughout church history have been closely associated with and woven into the warp and woof of the doctrine of the well-meant offer were already taught in the days of Augustine. These include the freedom of the will; a double will of God that desires the salvation of all men and wills the salvation of only the elect; a general grace that everyone receives and a special grace that is conditionally granted upon the choice of the will; and a general love of God for everyone that is expressed in God's desire to save everyone.

Augustine stood firm against all these views in his defense of sovereign grace. While his views did not prevail in his time or in subsequent centuries, they were once again made the confession of the church and developed during the sixteenth-century Reformation.

Those who teach a well-meant offer of the gospel will have to admit that they belong in the camp of the Pelagians and have no place at the side of Augustine.

Chapter 2

⎯⎯✦⎯⎯

MARTIN LUTHER AND JOHN CALVIN

The Middle Ages produced little of value regarding the well-meant offer. A brief mention of a few events will be sufficient.

The controversy between the followers of Augustine and the semi-Pelagians continued off and on for many years. The dispute came before several provincial synods, and the Synod of Valence in 855 even approved of Augustine's position. The Synod of Touchy in 860, the final synod to deal with the controversy, retracted the decisions of Valence and reiterated a Pelagian position.[1] The Roman Catholic Church was committed to the doctrines Augustine opposed: free will, the meritorious value of good works, God's love for all men, and a cross of Christ that had universal value—all the doctrines later associated with the error of the well-meant offer.

---

1 For a more detailed discussion of this history, see Herman Hanko, *Contending for the Faith: The Rise of Heresy and the Development of the Truth* (Jenison, MI: Reformed Free Publishing Association, 2010), 95–103.

Gottschalk (806–68) had discovered and defended the doctrines of Augustine and would not recant even under torture. He died a martyr's death at the hands of the cruel Roman Catholic Church.[2]

Another important viewpoint indirectly connected to the well-meant offer was Anselm's. Anselm (1033–1109) was the archbishop of Canterbury. He outlined a biblical position on the atonement.[3] The debate at that time was over the necessity of the atonement. In keeping with the view of the meritorious value of good works, most theologians held that the atonement was only relatively or partially necessary. The cross only supplied what good works could not accomplish. Anselm held to the doctrine of the absolute necessity of the atonement, a position he set forth in his book *Cur Deus Homo?* (Why did God become man?). Questions and answers 9–19 of the Heidelberg Catechism follow Anselm's line of argumentation.

Anselm's position was important, because he taught that only an absolute necessity of the atonement can be a basis for the sovereign and particular grace of salvation. The gospel proclaims to lost sinners what God has done in Christ, not what God has done supplemented by what man can do. The latter must be and is the position of those who hold to a well-meant offer, for God has done all he can to save everyone, but not everyone is saved. Anselm's work was a crucial step in the development of Augustine's doctrine of grace.

It ought not to come as a surprise that the well-meant offer

---

2   For his biography, see Herman Hanko, *Portraits of Faithful Saints* (Grandville, MI: Reformed Free Publishing Association, 1999), 68–72. See also Connie L. Meyer, *Gottschalk, Servant of God: A Story of Courage, Faith, and Love for the Truth* (Jenison, MI: Reformed Free Publishing Association, 2015).

3   For Anselm's life and beliefs see Hanko, *Portraits of Faithful Saints*, 73–78.

of the gospel was not an issue in the controversies between the reformers and the Roman Catholic Church. Their controversy did not concern the character and content of the preaching, which lie at the heart of the doctrine of the well-meant offer of the gospel. The reformers' controversy with Rome mostly concerned preaching as an integral and necessary part of the calling of the church.

Throughout the Middle Ages, with the growth of Rome's sacerdotalism and an increasingly strong emphasis on the mass, very little preaching was to be found in Roman Catholic worship services. If preaching was present, it was often little more than the recitation or reading of homilies from preachers of earlier ages. Expository preaching of the scriptures did not exist in most of the church of Rome prior to the Reformation.

The reformers without exception restored preaching to its rightful place in the worship services. That radical transformation of the worship services was a necessary consequence of the reformers' views of scripture and of the office of believer as it functioned within the church. When preaching was restored to its proper place, the reformers, guided exclusively by the Bible as the rule of faith and life, began anew a tradition of preaching that had existed in the church in her earliest New Testament history and that continued to be the distinguishing mark of all churches of the Reformation that remained faithful to their heritage. Since the Reformation, preaching is the outstanding feature of genuinely Protestant churches and has been the real and only strength of those churches for almost five hundred years.

If in today's ecclesiastical world radical changes are happening to the view of the place of preaching in the worship services, to the nature and character of the preaching, and to the contents of the preaching, this is because today's churches refuse to be faithful to their Reformation heritage and consciously depart from it.

In the consideration of the Pelagian and semi-Pelagian controversies, I mentioned that although the offer of the gospel was not one of the issues, doctrinal matters inseparably connected to the well-meant offer were faced. Some of the questions were the extent of the atonement, the particularity or universality of grace, the intention of God with respect to salvation—whether his intention is to save everyone or only those he has chosen—and the relationship between God's will of decree and God's will of command. These doctrinal questions were also considered at the time of the Reformation.

Although the Roman Catholic Church had adopted the semi-Pelagian position with respect to the extent of the atonement, that subject was not on the foreground during the battles of the first half of the sixteenth century. It seems from the literature that a particular atonement for the elect was simply assumed.

We must be careful, however, not to interpret the reformers and their views in the light of modern times and theological controversies. This is a great danger, whatever may be one's personal views of the well-meant offer. Everyone who appeals to the reformers, especially to Calvin, as their spiritual fathers ought to be honest enough not to put words in the mouths of the reformers and appeal unjustly to them in support of views that theologians now believe and cherish but that were far from the minds of those who brought reformation to the church in the sixteenth century. We can well bear in mind the remarks of William Cunningham (1805–61), a noted Scottish theologian who warned against this danger.

> In almost all theological controversies, much space has been occupied by the discussion of extracts from books and documents, adduced as authorities in support of the

opinions maintained; and there is certainly no department of theological literature in which so much ability and learning, so much time and strength, have been uselessly wasted, or in which so much of controversial unfairness has been exhibited. Controversialists in general have shown an intense and irresistible desire to prove, that their peculiar opinions were supported by the fathers, or by the Reformers, or by the great divines of their own church; and have often exhibited a great want both of wisdom and of candour in the efforts they have made to effect this object...

When men have never, or scarcely ever, had present to their thoughts the precise question that may have afterwards become a matter of dispute—when they have never deliberately examined it, or given a formal and explicit deliverance regarding it—it will usually follow, 1st, That it is difficult if not impossible to ascertain what they thought about it,—to collect this from incidental statements, or mere allusions, dropped when they were treating of other topics; and, 2d, That their opinion about it, if it could be ascertained, would be of no weight or value...The opinion even of Calvin, upon a point which he had never carefully examined, and on which he has given no formal deliverance, is of no weight or value, and would scarcely be worth examining...

In dealing with authorities, then, it is necessary to ascertain, whether the authors referred to and quoted have really formed and expressed an opinion upon the point, in regard to which their testimony is adduced. It is necessary further to collect together, and to examine carefully and deliberately, the whole of what they have written upon the subject under consideration, that we may understand fully and accurately what their whole mind regarding it really was, instead of trying to educe it from a hasty glance at partial and incidental statements.[4]

This is good and necessary advice.

I now turn to a brief consideration of Luther's views on the well-meant offer and related doctrines and the views of subsequent Lutheranism regarding them.

One can search Luther's writings in vain for references to either the well-meant offer of the gospel or to the doctrines related to the well-meant offer. There is no solid evidence that Luther wanted any part of these views. However, I came across one interesting passage in *The Bondage of the Will* that might at first glance suggest something similar to a well-meant offer.

> So it is right to say: "If God does not desire our death, it must be laid to the charge of our own will if we perish": this, I repeat, is right, if you spoke of God preached. For he desires that all men should be saved, in that He comes to all by the word of salvation, and the fault is in the will which does not receive Him; as He says in Matt. 23:[37].[5]

Although Luther expressed that God "desires that all men should be saved," there is no reference to the well-meant offer to all who hear the gospel. Luther's statement is found in a section of *The Bondage of the Will* in which he discussed the interpretation of Ezekiel 18:23, a passage to which Erasmus appealed in

---

4   William Cunningham, *The Reformers and the Theology of the Reformation* (Edinburgh: T. and T. Clark, 1863), 406–9.

5   Martin Luther, *The Bondage of the Will: A New Translation of* De Servo Arbitrio *(1525) Martin Luther's Reply to Erasmus of Rotterdam*, trans. J. I. Packer and O. R. Johnston (Old Tappan, NJ: Fleming H. Revell Company, 1957), 171.

support of the doctrine of free will. Erasmus argued that Ezekiel 18:23 teaches that God desires all men to be saved, and the fact that only some are saved shows that salvation rests on man's free will. Luther repudiated that interpretation with all his soul and insisted that when God asks, "Have I any pleasure at all that the wicked should die?" this is a promise of God, found in "more than half the Holy Scriptures," that is intended to comfort the hearts of those who are troubled by their sins and fearful of the wrath of an almighty God.[6] Such persons, said Luther, are already saved by the power of God's grace in their hearts, because the law has brought them sorrow for sins and fears of death, and therefore the promises of the gospel are worked in them.[7] Luther explained why some are so affected by the law and others are not.

> As to why some are touched by the law and others not, so that some receive and others scorn the offer of grace, that is another question, which Ezekiel does not here discuss. He speaks of the published offer of God's mercy, not of the dreadful hidden will of God, Who, according to His own counsel, ordains such persons as He wills to receive and partake of the mercy preached and offered. This will is not to be inquired into, but to be reverently adored, as by far the most awesome secret of the Divine Majesty. He has kept it to Himself and forbidden us to know it; and it is much more worthy of reverence than an infinite number of Corycian caverns![8]

It is clear from all this that Luther interpreted Ezekiel 18:23

---

6   Ibid., 166–68.
7   Ibid., 169.
8   Ibid.

CORRUPTING THE WORD OF GOD

as referring to God's people alone. This is striking, since it is one of the scriptural passages that the defenders of the well-meant offer often appeal to in support of their view. Luther did not teach that this passage must be interpreted to mean that God wants all men to be saved.

Not only was Luther very strongly opposed throughout *The Bondage of the Will* to the idea of God's desire to save all men, but he also was strong on the doctrines of the particularity of the atonement and of grace and the harmony between the hidden and revealed wills of God. All his writings that deal with these subjects reflect that emphasis.

Luther did not have the insipid idea of preaching that defenders of the well-meant offer have today. He considered the preaching of the gospel to be the great power to save. In a sermon he said, "I simply taught, preached, wrote God's Word; otherwise I did nothing. And then, while I slept, or drank Wittenberg beer with my Philip and my Amsdorf, the Word so greatly weakened the papacy that never a prince or emperor did such damage to it. I did nothing. The Word did it all."[9] A well-meant offer cannot do these things.

Lutheranism did not remain in that tradition in large measure due to the influence of Philip Melanchthon, Luther's co-worker and fellow reformer. It is well known that especially after Luther's death Melanchthon drifted away from the strong and sharp truths of sovereign grace as maintained by Luther. In the place of sovereign grace Melanchthon introduced into Lutheran thinking a synergism that taught that salvation was the cooperative work of God and man. This weakness in later

---

9   Martin Luther, "Sermon on Monday after Invocavit" (March 10, 1522), in *Luther's Works*, American Edition, ed. Jaroslav Pelikan and Helmut T. Lehmann (Philadelphia: Muehlenberg and Fortress and St. Louis: Concordia, 1955–86), 51:77.

Lutheranism is reflected in the Lutheran confessions, particularly in the Formula of Concord (1576). Article 11, dealing with the subject of eternal predestination, states:

> But Christ calls all sinners to him, and promises to give them rest. And he earnestly wishes that all men may come to him, and suffer themselves to be cared for and succored. To these he offers himself in the Word as a Redeemer, and wishes that the Word may be heard, and that their ears may not be hardened, nor the Word be neglected and contemned. And he promises that he will bestow the virtue and operation of the Holy Spirit and divine aid, to the end that we may abide steadfast in the faith and attain eternal life.[10]

> But as to the declaration (Matt. 22:14), "Many are called, but few are chosen," it is not to be so understood as if God were unwilling that all should be saved, but the cause of the damnation of the ungodly is that they either do not hear the Word of God at all, but contumaciously contemn it, stop their ears, and harden their hearts, and in this way foreclose to the Spirit of God his ordinary way, so that he cannot accomplish his work in them, or at least when they have heard the Word, make it of no account, and cast it away. Neither God nor his election, but their own wickedness, is to blame if they perish (2 Pet. 2:1ff.; Luke 2:49, 52; Heb. 12:25ff.).[11]

These ideas in the Formula of Concord come out even more

---

10 Formula of Concord 11.7, affirmative, in Philip Schaff, ed., *The Creeds of Christendom with a History and Critical Notes*, 6th ed., 3 vols. (New York: Harper and Row, 1931; repr., Grand Rapids, MI: Baker Books, 2007), 3:167.
11 Formula of Concord 11.11, affirmative, in ibid., 3:168–69.

strongly in the negative section of article 11, which reject the following errors:

I. That God is unwilling that all men should repent and believe the Gospel.

II. That when God calls us to him, he does not earnestly wish that all men should come to him.

III. That God is not willing that all should be saved, but that some men are destined to destruction, not on account of their sins, but by the mere counsel, purpose, and will of God, so that they can not in any wise attain to salvation.[12]

Luther would have violently disagreed that these statements are errors. The theology of the well-meant offer does not appear as an integral part of Luther's thought, but as a doctrinal formulation brought into Lutheranism under the weakening influence of Melanchthon's synergism.

It is not my purpose to enter into detail regarding the teachings of John Calvin on the subject of the well-meant offer. Much ink has been spilled, much fierce argumentation has echoed in ecclesiastical halls, and much disagreement has torn apart Reformed believers on this question. This relatively short discussion of Calvin's views is justified on three grounds.

First, although there are innumerable passages in Calvin's writings where he used the word *offer*, the actual theology of the well-meant offer was a subject that Calvin did not face. The issue of the well-meant offer arose over a half-century later. Therefore, to interpret Calvin in the light of subsequent controversies over the well-meant offer is to read into Calvin something that is not

---

12 Formula of Concord 11.1–3, negative, in ibid., 3:171–72.

there. I remind the reader of the warnings of William Cunningham quoted earlier.

Second, it is clear from Calvin's writings as a whole that he militated against all the ideas that have become such an integral part of well-meant-offer theology. I intend to show this briefly, but it can safely be said that every one of the doctrines that form a part of the teachings of the well-meant offer is expressly and specifically refuted by Calvin at one point or another in his writings. Taking all of Calvin's views and the whole genius of his theology into account, one can only conclude that present-day ideas of the well-meant offer were foreign to Calvin's thinking. The most that can be said is that in some respects Calvin used ambiguous language, especially if one is determined to weigh his language in the light of subsequent theological discussions.

Third, others have written on this subject and proved beyond doubt that Calvin wanted no part of what today goes under the name of the well-meant offer of the gospel.[13]

Concerning Calvin's use of the term *offer*, I agree with what David Engelsma wrote.

> It is of no consequence, therefore, that the term *offer* appears in Calvin, in other Reformed theologians, and the Canons of Dordt and the Westminster Confession of Faith. The word *offer* had originally a sound meaning: "serious call," "presentation of Christ." I am

---

13 See Herman Hoeksema, *Calvin, Berkhof and H. J. Kuiper: A Comparison* (Grand Rapids, MI: n.p., 1930). This work has been published in Henry Danhof and Herman Hoeksema, *The Rock Whence We Are Hewn: God, Grace, and Covenant*, ed. David J. Engelsma (Jenison, MI: Reformed Free Publishing Association, 2015), 291–347. See also Herman Hoeksema, *Een Kracht Gods Tot Zaligheid, of Genade Geen Aanbod* [The power of God unto salvation, or grace no offer], 2nd ed. (Grand Rapids, MI: Reformed Free Publishing Association, 1931).

fundamentally uninterested in warring over words. No, but I am interested to ask concerning the *doctrine* of the offer: is it Reformed?[14]

To demonstrate the contention that Calvin inveighed against all doctrines associated with the well-meant offer, I quote several passages from Calvin's writings:

> It is objected by some, that God will be inconsistent with himself, if he invites all men universally to come to him, and receives only a few elect. Thus, according to them, the universality of the promises destroys the discrimination of special grace…How the Scripture reconciles these two facts, that by external preaching all are called to repentance and faith, and yet that the spirit of repentance and faith is not given to all, I have elsewhere stated, and shall soon have occasion partly to repeat. What they assume, I deny as being false in two respects. For he who threatens drought in one city while it rains upon another, and who denounces to another place a famine of doctrine, lays himself under no positive obligation to call all men alike. And he who, forbidding Paul to preach the word in Asia, and suffering him not to go into Bithynia, calls him into Macedonia, demonstrates his right to distribute this treasure to whom he pleases. In Isaiah, he still more fully declares his destination of the promises of salvation exclusively for the elect; for of them only, and not indiscriminately of all mankind, he declares that they shall be his disciples [Isa. 8:16].

---

14 David J. Engelsma, *Hyper-Calvinism and the Call of the Gospel: An Examination of the Well-Meant Offer of the Gospel*, 3rd ed. (Jenison, MI: Reformed Free Publishing Association, 2014), 130.

Whence it appears, that when the doctrine of salvation is offered to all for their effectual benefit, it is a corrupt prostitution of that which is declared to be reserved particularly for the children of the church.[15]

To a further elucidation of the subject, it is necessary to treat of the calling of the elect, and of the blinding and hardening of the impious. On the former I have already made a few observations, with a view to refute the error of those who suppose the generality of the promises to put all mankind on an equality. But the discriminating election of God, which is otherwise concealed within himself, he manifests only by his calling, which may therefore with propriety be termed the testification or evidence of it.[16]

Calvin continued and showed that the scriptures teach a perfect unity between the truth of sovereign election and the calling of the gospel. He spoke in more than one place of the sovereign purpose of God in the preaching of the gospel to harden the reprobate.

The declaration of Christ, that "many are called, and few chosen," is very improperly understood. For there will be no ambiguity in it, if we remember what must be clear from the foregoing observations, that there are two kinds of calling. For there is a universal call, by which God, in the external preaching of the word, invites all, indiscriminately, to come to him, *even those to whom he*

---

15 John Calvin, *Institutes of the Christian Religion*, trans. John Allen (Grand Rapids, MI: Wm. B. Eerdmans Publishing Company, 1949), 3.22.10, 2:194-45.

16 Ibid., 3.24.1, 2:217.

intends it as a savour of death, and an occasion of heavier condemnation.[17]

As the Lord, by his effectual calling of the elect, completes the salvation to which he predestinated them in his eternal counsel, so he has his judgments against the reprobate, by which he executes his counsel respecting them. Those, therefore, whom he has created to a life of shame and a death of destruction, that they might be instruments of his wrath, and examples of his severity, he causes to reach their appointed end, sometimes depriving them of the opportunity of hearing the word, *sometimes, by the preaching of it, increasing their blindness and stupidity.*[18]

Why, then, in bestowing grace upon some, does he pass over others? Luke assigns a reason for the former, that they "were ordained to eternal life." What conclusion, then, shall we draw respecting the latter, but that they are vessels of wrath to dishonour?...It is a fact not to be doubted, that God sends his word to many whose blindness he determines shall be increased. For with what design does he direct so many commands to be delivered to Pharaoh? Was it from an expectation that his heart would be softened by repeated and frequent messages? Before he began, he knew and foretold the result. He commanded Moses to go and declare his will to Pharaoh, adding at the same time, "But I will harden his heart, that he shall not let the people go" [Ex. 4:21].[19]

---

17 Ibid., 3.24.8, 2:227; emphasis added.
18 Ibid., 3.24.12, 2:232; emphasis added.
19 Ibid., 3.24.13, 2:233–34.

Calvin also wrote concerning Ezekiel 33:11, a passage often referred to by defenders of the well-meant offer of the gospel.

As objections are frequently raised from some passages of Scripture, in which God seems to deny that the destruction of the wicked is caused by his decree, but that, in opposition to his remonstrances, they voluntarily bring ruin upon themselves—let us show by a brief explication that they are not at all inconsistent with the foregoing doctrine. A passage is produced from Ezekiel, where God says, "I have no pleasure in the death of the wicked, but that the wicked turn from his way and live" [33:11]. If this is to be extended to all mankind, why does he not urge many to repentance, whose minds are more flexible to obedience than those of others, who grow more and more callous to his daily invitations? Among the inhabitants of Nineveh and Sodom, Christ himself declares that his evangelical preaching and miracles would have brought forth more fruit than in Judea. How is it, then, if God will have all men to be saved, that he opens not the gate of repentance to those miserable men who would be more ready to receive the favour? Hence we perceive it to be a violent perversion of the passage, if the will of God, mentioned by the prophet, be set in opposition to his eternal counsel, by which he has distinguished the elect from the reprobate. Now if we inquire the genuine sense of the prophet, his only meaning is to inspire the penitent with hopes of pardon. And this is the sum, that it is beyond a doubt that God is ready to pardon sinners immediately on their conversion. Therefore he wills not their death, inasmuch as he wills their repentance. But experience teaches, that he does not will the repentance of those whom he externally calls, in such a manner as to affect all their hearts. Nor should he on this account be charged with acting deceitfully; for, though his external call only renders those who hear without obeying it inexcusable, yet it is justly esteemed the testimony of God's grace, by which he reconciles men to himself. Let us observe, therefore, the design of the prophet in saying that God has no pleasure in the death of a sinner; it is to assure the pious of God's readiness to pardon them immediately on their repentance, and to show the impious the aggravation of their sin in rejecting such great compassion and kindness of God. Repentance, therefore, will always be met by Divine mercy; but on whom repentance is bestowed, we are clearly taught by Ezekiel himself, as well as by all the prophets and apostles.[20]

While I could multiply similar passages from the *Institutes*, I turn now to Calvin's treatise on "God's Eternal Predestination and Secret Providence." Calvin wrote the treatise during his second stay in Geneva, particularly in connection with the Bolsec controversy. Jerome Bolsec had disrupted the ecclesiastical life of Geneva with sometimes violent attacks against the truth of sovereign predestination. Calvin's treatise was sent to other Protestant cantons in Switzerland, but it never received their full approval. However, it had the united support of the Genevan pastors. Therefore, it has become known as the *Consensus Genevensis* (Consent of the pastors of the church in Geneva). It is the fruit of many years of study and is perhaps Calvin's clearest

---

20 Ibid., 3.24.15, 2:236–37. Some might object that Calvin used the word "invitations," which has the implication of the right to accept or reject. But an invitation from a king is a command that men refuse at their peril.

statement on the truths of sovereign predestination and providence.

All this Pighius[21] loudly denies, citing the passage of the apostle Paul, "Who will have all men to be saved" (1 Tim. 2:4). Referring also to Ezekiel 18:23, Pighius argues thus: That God wills not the death of a sinner may be taken upon his own oath, where he says by that prophet, "As I live, saith the Lord, I have no pleasure in death of the wicked; but rather that he should return from his way and live" (Ezek. 33:11)...In the same manner God declared to the Ninevites, and to the kings of Gerar and Egypt, that he would do what in reality he did not intend to do, for their repentance averted the punishment that he had threatened to inflict upon them...But after God had terrified them with the apprehension of his wrath and had duly humbled them as not being utterly desperate, he encourages them with the hope of pardon, that they might feel that there was yet left open a space for remedy. Just so it is with respect to the conditional promises of God that invite all men to salvation. They do not positively prove what God has decreed in his secret counsel, but declare only what God is ready to do to all those who are brought to faith and repentance.[22]

It is obvious that Calvin referred to the command of the gospel to repent and believe in Christ, which comes to all men who

---

21 Pighius, a Roman Catholic opponent of Calvin, hated Calvin's doctrine of sovereign predestination.

22 John Calvin, *Calvin's Calvinism: God's Eternal Predestination and Secret Providence* together with *A Brief Reply* and *Reply to the Slanderous Reports*, trans. Henry Cole, ed. Russell J. Dykstra, 2nd ed. (Jenison, MI: Reformed Free Publishing Association, 2009), 87–88.

hear the gospel. But a command is not a well-meant offer. Calvin continued:

> But men untaught of God, not understanding these things, allege that we hereby attribute to God a twofold or double will, whereas God is so far from being variable that no shadow of such variableness appertains to him, even in the most remote degree. Hence Pighius, ignorant of the divine nature of these deep things, thus argues, "What else is this but making God a mocker of men if God is represented as really not willing what he professes to will, and as not having pleasure in what he actually has pleasure?" But if these two parts of the sentence be read in conjunction, as they ought to be—"*I have no pleasure in the death of the wicked,*" and "*but that the wicked turn from his way and live*"(Ezek. 33:11)—the calumny is washed off at once. God requires of us this conversion, or turning away from our iniquity (Ezek. 18:23, 30; Ezek. 33:11), and in whomever he finds it, he does not disappoint such a one of the promised reward of eternal life. Therefore, God is as much said to have pleasure in and to will this eternal life as to have pleasure in repentance; he has pleasure in repentance because he invites all men to it by his word. All this is in perfect harmony with his secret and eternal counsel by which he decreed to convert none except his own elect. None but God's elect, therefore, ever do turn from their wickedness. Yet on these accounts the adorable God is not to be considered variable or capable of change, because as a lawgiver he enlightens all man with the external doctrine of conditional life. In this primary manner he calls or invites all men unto eternal life. But he brings unto

eternal life his own children, only those whom he willed according to his eternal purpose and regenerated by his Spirit as an eternal Father.

It is quite certain that men do not "turn from their evil ways" to the Lord of their own accord or by any instinct of nature. Equally certain is it that the gift of conversion is not common to all men; because this is one of the two covenants that God promises he will not make with any but his own children and his own elect people, concerning whom he has recorded his promise, "I will write my law in their hearts" (Jer. 31:33). A man must be utterly beside himself to assert that this promise is made to all men generally and indiscriminately.[23]

Calvin insisted that while the preaching of the gospel must and does come to all men with the command to repent and believe, through the command God sovereignly accomplishes his eternal decree of election and reprobation.

It is clear from these quotations that Calvin expressly repudiated the theology of the well-meant offer of the gospel.

Universal atonement is another doctrine that has become an important part of well-meant-offer theology. It is maintained today that Calvin taught universal atonement. Various references in Calvin's writings are often quoted to substantiate this view.

That universal atonement is closely connected to the well-meant offer of the gospel is evident from the fact that wherever the well-meant offer of the gospel is taught, universal atonement

---

23 Ibid., 88–89. Calvin's use of *conditional* is not to be construed as referring to a condition or prerequisite that man must fulfill before God can act. Rather, it is a way of designating the *means* God sovereignly uses to save or to harden.

has become an inseparable companion doctrine. Those who wish to remain identified as Calvinists in distinction from Arminians will point out that they do not believe in the universal *efficacy* of the atonement. But they will still defend universal atonement with respect to its *sufficiency* and almost always with respect to its *intention* and *availability*.

It is easy to see that these ideas constitute important aspects of the idea of the offer. If God through the preaching truly expresses his desire and intention to save everyone who hears the preaching, this expression of God's desire and intention can be serious and well-meant only if in some sense salvation is available to everyone who hears the gospel. By the implications of the well-meant offer, those who adopt such a view are driven inevitably to a universal view of the death of Christ.

The often-debated question is, did Calvin teach universal atonement? Cunningham has an interesting discussion of that subject.

It has been contended very frequently, and very confidently, that Calvin did not sanction the views which have been generally held by Calvinistic divines, in regard to the extent of the atonement,—that he did not believe in the doctrine of particular redemption, that is, that Christ did not die for all men, but only for the elect, and for those who are actually saved,—but that, on the contrary, he asserted a universal, unlimited, or indefinite atonement. Amyraut, in defending his doctrine of universal atonement in combination with Calvinistic views upon other points, appealed confidently to the authority of Calvin...

It is certain that Beza held the doctrine of particular redemption, or of a limited atonement, as it has since been held by most Calvinists, and brought it out fully in his controversies with the Lutherans on the subject of predestination; though he was not, as has sometimes been asserted, the first who maintained it. It has been confidently alleged that Calvin did not concur in this view, but held the opposite doctrine of universal redemption and unlimited atonement...

There is not, then, we are persuaded, satisfactory evidence that Calvin held the doctrine of a universal, unlimited, or indefinite atonement...The evidence of this position is derived chiefly from the following two considerations.

1st. Calvin consistently, unhesitatingly, and explicitly denied the doctrine of God's universal grace and love to all men—that is, *omnibus et singulis,* to each and every man,—as implying in some sense a desire or purpose or intention to save them all; and with this universal grace or love to all men the doctrine of a universal or unlimited atonement, in the nature of the case, and in the convictions and admissions of all its supporters, stands inseparably connected. That Calvin denied the doctrine of God's universal grace or love to all men, as implying some desire or intention of saving them all, and some provision directed to that object, is too evident to any one who has read his writings, to admit of doubt or to require proof...And then this conclusion warrants us in maintaining, that the fact of Calvin so explicitly denying the doctrine of God's universal grace or love to all men, affords a more direct and certain ground for the inference, that he did not hold the doctrine of universal atonement, than could be legitimately deduced from the mere fact, that he held the doctrine of unconditional

personal election to everlasting life. The invalidity of
the inferential process in the one case is not sufficient
to establish its invalidity in the other; and therefore our
argument holds good.[24]

I am in complete agreement with Cunningham's important
statement. While proving that in Calvin's writings there is abun-
dant proof that Calvin did not hold to the doctrine of universal
atonement, Cunningham made several other important observations.

First, he correctly insisted that Calvin "consistently, unhesitatingly, and explicitly denied the doctrine of God's universal
grace and love to all men."

Second, he pointed out that Calvin in no sense taught a
desire, purpose, or intention of God to save all men, an idea that
is the heart of the theology of the well-meant offer. In fact, Cunningham insisted that he could rest his case concerning Calvin's
denial of universal atonement on Calvin's repudiation of the
entire idea of an offer. How much more strongly can it be put?
That Calvin denied all that is "too evident to any one who has
read his writings, to admit of doubt or to require proof." Cunningham understood Calvin. Would that modern defenders
of the well-meant offer had the same clear conception of what
Calvin taught. History has proved Cunningham correct that the
idea of a well-meant offer of the gospel is inseparably connected
with the idea of a general grace and love of God to all men and a
universal atonement accomplished by Jesus Christ.

Third, Cunningham further proved his thesis that Calvin repudiated universal atonement by quoting from Calvin's
commentary on 1 Timothy 2:4 and 1 John 2:2. Cunningham's

---

24 Cunningham, *Reformers and the Theology of the Reformation*, 395–99.

argument was that Calvin "interpreted some of the principal texts on which the advocates of that doctrine rest it, in such a way as to deprive them of all capacity of serving the purpose to which its supporters commonly apply them."[25]

I give below the pertinent quotations from Calvin's commentaries rather than from Cunningham's book, because he quoted them in Latin. Also, I quote only those portions of Calvin's remarks on 1 John 2:2 that Cunningham quoted.

On 1 Timothy 2:4 Calvin wrote the following:

> The Apostle simply means, that there is no people and no rank in the world that is excluded from salvation; because God wishes that the gospel should be proclaimed to all without exception...But the present discourse relates to classes of men, and not to individual persons; for his sole object is, to include in this number princes and foreign nations.[26]

Concerning 1 John 2:2 Calvin wrote the following:

> Here a question may be raised, how have the sins of the whole world been expiated? I pass by the dotages of the fanatics, who under this pretence extend salvation to all the reprobate, and therefore to Satan himself. Such a monstrous thing deserves no refutation. They who seek to avoid this absurdity, have said that Christ suffered sufficiently for the whole world, but efficiently only for the elect. This solution has commonly prevailed in the

---

25 Ibid., 399–400.
26 John Calvin, *Commentaries on the Epistles to Timothy, Titus, and Philemon,* trans. William Pringle (Grand Rapids, MI: Baker Book House Company, repr., 1979), 54–55.

CORRUPTING THE WORD OF GOD

schools. Though then I allow that what has been said is true, yet I deny that it is suitable to this passage; for the design of John was no other than to make this benefit common to the whole Church. Then under the word *all* or whole, he does not include the reprobate, but designates those who should believe as well as those who were then scattered through various parts of the world. For then is really made evident, as it is meet, the grace of Christ, when it is declared to be the only true salvation of the world.[27]

Cunningham concluded his discussion of this subject with these remarks:

He [Calvin] gives the very same explanation of these two passages in his treatise on "Predestination." Now this is in substance just the interpretation commonly given of these and similar texts, by the advocates of the doctrine of particular redemption; and it seems scarcely possible, that it should have been adopted by one who did not hold that doctrine, or who believed in the truth of the opposite one.[28]

From all this it is clear that Calvin did not teach the doctrines that form an inseparable part of the well-meant offer of the gospel and that he was at great pains to contradict such doctrines and refute them with the power of the scriptures. Anyone who has read Calvin will have to admit that efforts to appeal to him in support of the well-meant offer are useless.

Several conclusions regarding Calvin can be drawn.

---

27 John Calvin, *Commentaries on the Catholic Epistles*, trans. and ed. John Owen (Grand Rapids, MI: Baker Book House Company; repr., 1979), 173.
28 Cunningham, *Reformers and the Theology of the Reformation*, 400.

He repeatedly used the word *offer* and by it often meant to express that Christ, in whom alone is salvation, is presented to men through the preaching of the gospel. Calvin emphasized very strongly that through the general proclamation of the gospel to all men, the command also comes to all men to repent of sin, to turn from evil, and to believe in Christ. With respect to the *doctrines* of the offer, Calvin's theology repeatedly militated against the offer.

Nor did Calvin want any part of a double will in God that conflicts with itself, according to which God determines to save only his elect and wills to save everyone. Cunningham was right: Calvin wanted nothing of a universal love or grace of God that is shown to all men. Perhaps passages can be quoted here and there in Calvin's writings to suggest that, but Calvin's *theology* militates against it.

Finally, while Calvin did not write at length on the extent of the atonement, what he wrote showed conclusively that he taught limited atonement for the elect only.

Calvin excluded himself from the company of defenders of the well-meant offer and did so by harshly condemning those who teach it.

Chapter 3

THE ARMINIAN CONTROVERSY AND THE SYNOD OF DORDRECHT

The Arminian controversy that raged in the churches of the Netherlands during the last part of the sixteenth century and the early part of the seventeenth century did not deal directly with the well-meant offer of the gospel. Nevertheless, there are two reasons that a consideration of that controversy is important for a discussion of the history of the well-meant offer.

First, in the defense of their position, the Arminians raised many of the identical issues that repeatedly have been raised in discussions of the well-meant offer. Especially in their views of the preaching and the relationship between the preaching and the atonement, the Arminians set forth ideas that have been inextricably woven into the well-meant-offer concept.

Second, although the Canons of Dordt were written against Arminian heresies, the Canons repeatedly have been appealed to, especially in Dutch Reformed theology, in support of the well-meant offer. In fact, in its decisions on common grace taken in 1924, the Christian Reformed Church appealed to Canons 2.5 and 3-4.8-9 as confessional proof for the doctrine of the well-meant offer.

Especially three Arminian heresies are related to the well-meant offer.

First, the Arminians taught a certain common grace of God that is imparted to all men. While many who stand in the tradition of Dordt also teach common grace and even appeal to the Canons to support their views, the term "common grace" appears in the Canons only in the mouths of the Arminians, where it is condemned. That common grace was equated with the light of nature, which constitutes the gifts left in man after the fall. The Synod of Dordt rejected the error of those

> who teach that the corrupt and natural man can so well use the common grace (by which they understand the light of nature), or the gifts still left him after the fall, that he can gradually gain by their good use a greater, namely, the evangelical or saving grace and salvation itself. And that in this way God on his part shows himself ready to reveal Christ unto all men, since he applies to all sufficiently and efficiently the means necessary to conversion.[1]

The Arminians said the light of nature shows God ready to reveal Christ to all men and sufficiently and efficiently to apply to all men the means necessary to receive Christ, to believe, and to repent. Thus one must rightly use the light of nature to become worthy of saving grace. At that point the Arminians introduced the idea of free will, so that the salvation of man is in the end dependent on the exercise of man's free will.

---

1 Canons of Dordt 3-4, error 5, in *Confessions and Church Order*, 171.

This same view, taught by the Arminians and condemned by the fathers at Dordt, has reappeared in Reformed theology in connection with an identification of general revelation and common grace. William Masselink and Herman Bavinck taught this.[2]

Second, the Arminians taught a governmental and universalistic view of the atonement and held that in every sense the atonement is for every individual person. However, they said that atonement only makes salvation available and possible for all. Thus they denied the efficacy of the atonement. The Synod of Dordt rejected the following Arminian errors:

That it was not the purpose of the death of Christ that he should confirm the new covenant of grace through his blood, but only that he should acquire for the Father the mere right to establish with man such a covenant as he might please, whether of grace or of works.

That Christ, by his satisfaction, merited neither salvation itself for anyone, nor faith, whereby this satisfaction of Christ unto salvation is effectually appropriated; but that he merited for the Father only the authority or the perfect will to deal again with man, and to prescribe new conditions as he might desire, obedience to which, however, depended on the free will of man, so that it therefore might have come to pass that either none or all should fulfill these conditions.

That all men have been accepted unto the state of reconciliation and unto the grace of the covenant, so that no one is worthy of condemnation on account of original

---

2   See William Masselink, *General Revelation and Common Grace*. See also Bavinck, *Our Reasonable Faith*, 32–60.

sin, and that no one shall be condemned because of it, but that all are free from the guilt of original sin.[3]

Third, in connection with these views, the Arminians promoted a particular view of preaching. They challenged the Reformed position and said that the Reformed could not really preach because they preach only to the elect, but they do not know who the elect are. This objection of the Arminians against the Reformed is the same as is repeatedly hurled by the defenders of the well-meant offer against those who oppose this heresy. The Arminians also claimed that the Reformed cannot preach faith and repentance as the general command of the gospel. The views of these Arminians are set forth in their writings and in "The Opinions of the Remonstrants," which is a statement of their convictions regarding the points in dispute at the Synod of Dordt, and which they were required to submit to the synod. The Remonstrants' opinion regarding the universality of the merit of the death of Christ is as follows:

> Only those are obliged to believe that Christ died for them for whom Christ has died. The reprobates, however, as they are called, for whom Christ has not died, are not obligated to such faith, nor can they be justly condemned on account of the contrary refusal to believe this. In fact, if there should be such reprobates, they would be obliged to believe that Christ has not died for them.[4]

---

3 Canons of Dordt 2, errors 2–3, 5, in *Confessions and Church Order*, 164–65.
4 "The Opinions of the Remonstrants" B.4, trans. Anthony A. Hoekema, in Peter Y. De Jong, ed., *Crisis in the Reformed Churches: Essays in Commemoration of the Great Synod of Dort, 1618–1619* (Grand Rapids, MI: Reformed Fellowship, Inc., 1968), 225. The Dutch translation of all the Remonstrants' Opinions is found in *Acta ofte Handelinghen des Nationalen Synodi* (ed. Canin, 1621), 138–39, 152–58.

This article by the Arminian delegation at Dordt was intended to show the foolishness of the Reformed position, which they caricatured. Written with characteristic vagueness, it supposedly proved that the Reformed, who insisted that scripture taught atonement only for the elect, could not confront all men with the command to repent and believe. The reprobate cannot be commanded to repent and believe in Christ, it was argued, for they would be required to believe something that would not be true, namely, that Christ died for them. The Arminians stated their position this way:

> Whomever God calls to salvation, he calls seriously, that is, with a sincere and completely unhypocritical intention and will to save; nor do we assent to the opinion of those who hold that God calls certain ones externally whom He does not will to call internally, that is, as truly converted, even before the grace of calling has been rejected.[5]

The Arminians specifically stated as their position that God calls all men with the will and purpose to save all, and they disagreed with those who teach that God does not will the conversion of all those who are externally called, at least not if the will of God precedes the rejection of the gospel by the wicked. This is a clear statement of the Arminian conception of the theology of the well-meant offer. In their Opinions the Arminians also stated that

> there is not in God a secret will which so contradicts the will of the same revealed in the Word that according to it (that is, the secret will) He does not will the

---

5 "The Opinions of the Remonstrants" C.8, in ibid., 226–27.

conversion and salvation of the greatest part of those whom He seriously calls and invites by the Word of the Gospel and by His revealed will; and we do not here, as some say, acknowledge in God a holy dissimulation, or a double person.[6]

Calvin taught that according to his hidden will, God wills the salvation of the elect, and that, although God commands everyone who hears the gospel to repent and believe, there is no conflict between God's will revealed in his word and his hidden will. Modern-day defenders of the well-meant offer of the gospel insist that according to his hidden will, God desires and wills the salvation only of the elect, but that according to his revealed will, he desires and wills the salvation of all men. They say that although the two wills are seemingly contradictory, they are not so in the mind of God, and this remains a mystery. The Arminians also insisted that there is no conflict between God's hidden will and his revealed will; they found the harmony of the two by teaching that according to both God seriously desires and wills the salvation of all men.

According to the Arminians, all of these ideas are rooted in the universal atoning sacrifice of Jesus Christ.

The price of redemption which Christ offered to God the Father is not only in itself and by itself sufficient for the redemption of the whole human race but has also been paid for all men and for every man, according to the decree, will, and grace of God the Father; therefore no one is absolutely excluded from participation in the fruits of Christ's death by an absolute and antecedent decree of God.[7]

---

6 "The Opinions of the Remonstrants" C.9, in ibid., 227.
7 "The Opinions of the Remonstrants" B.1, in ibid., 224.

The Arminians made the following points at Dordt: salvation is offered to all men without exception in the preaching of the gospel; God desires to save all men, as expressed in the offer;[8] this offer is rooted in an unlimited atonement for every and all men; and the acceptance or rejection of this offer depends on the free will of man. The fathers at Dordt rejected the errors

> of those who use the difference between meriting and appropriating, to the end that they may instill into the minds of the imprudent and inexperienced this teaching, *that God, as far as he is concerned, has been minded of applying to all equally the benefits gained by the death of Christ;* but that, while some obtain the pardon of sin and eternal life and others do not, *this difference depends on their own free will, which joins itself to the grace that is offered without exception,* and that it is not dependent on the special gift of mercy, which powerfully works in them, that they rather than others should appropriate unto themselves this grace.[9]

---

8 There is always some ambiguity in connection with this point. The well-meant offer of the gospel teaches that God expresses his desire to save all those who hear the gospel, for the gospel itself is the means God uses to make his desire known. At the same time, it is clear from the statement on the offer, and particularly in the Christian Reformed Church's first point of common grace, that God desires the salvation of all men whether they hear the gospel or not. He is gracious to all men, as is evident from the offer of the gospel. How God expresses his desire to save all those who do not hear the gospel is an unanswered question. Presumably, the answer is that God's speech in creation, such as in rain and sunshine, indicate God's love for those who have never heard the gospel.

9 Canons of Dordt 2, error 6, in *Confessions and Church Order*, 166; emphasis added.

The free will taught by the Arminians involved an exercise of faith that they considered to be the work of man. This error was also pointed out in the Canons:

> Faith is...to be considered as the gift of God, not on account of its being offered by God to man, to be accepted or rejected at his pleasure, but because it is in reality conferred, breathed, and infused into him; or even because God bestows the power or ability to believe, and then expects that man should by the exercise of his own free will consent to the terms of salvation and actually believe in Christ, but because he who works in man both to will and to do, and indeed all things in all, produces both the will to believe and the act of believing also.[10]

It is not surprising, then, that for the Arminians the preaching of the gospel is not the power of God unto salvation (Rom. 1:16), but is only God's attempt to persuade the sinner to accept Christ and to walk in obedience. That this was the teaching of the Arminians at Dordt is evident from the fathers' rejection of the error of those who teach

> that the grace whereby we are converted to God is only a gentle advising, or (as others explain it) that this is the noblest manner of working in the conversion of man, and that this manner of working, which consists in advising, is most in harmony with man's nature; and that there is no reason why this advising grace alone should not be sufficient to make the natural man spiritual, indeed, that God does not produce the consent of the will except

---

10 Canons of Dordt 3–4.14, in ibid., 169.

through this manner of advising; and that the power of the divine working, whereby it surpasses the working of Satan, consists in this, that God promises eternal, while Satan promises only temporal goods.[11]

From this it is clear that the Arminians of the seventeenth century, while not teaching the offer in exactly the same form as it is taught today, nevertheless held to the same related doctrines as those who maintain a well-meant offer of the gospel.

It is well to remember that the Canons were the product of the entire Reformed church world of 1619 and were signed by all the delegates, both foreign and within the Netherlands, where the synod was held. A clearer confessional condemnation of the doctrines of the well-meant offer can hardly be found. Dordt's condemnation of the Arminian position was the united opinion of all the churches of the Reformation at that time.

What makes this more important is that certain delegates from foreign countries, especially from England and Bremen, Germany, defended the Arminian position on the floor of the synod. Although it is true that they also subsequently signed the Canons, it is difficult to imagine how that was possible since they consistently upheld the Arminian position. However, the point is that the Arminian viewpoint was given a hearing at the synod, not only when the Arminians were permitted to speak, but also through the defense of the Arminian position by the delegates from Great Britain and Bremen. In spite of that, the fathers refused to adopt any Arminian views and consistently repudiated them.

The Arminian position was fundamentally rationalistic. It was a theological system that involved almost all points of doctrine.

---

11 Canons of Dordt 3–4, error 7, in ibid., 172.

It proceeded from a rationalistic starting point and by rationalistic deduction demonstrated that departure in one element of the truth leads to departure in every part of it.

The Arminianism condemned at Dordt was somewhat different from Wesleyan Arminianism that appeared later in England. In an interesting paper, J. I. Packer correctly characterized Wesleyan Arminianism as pietistic and never fully developed into a theological system. Nevertheless, as Packer also noted, the basic ideas of both types of Arminianism are the same.[12]

We ought to face two matters in a discussion of the Canons of Dordt. Sometimes it is maintained that Canons 2.3 is the only place the fathers of Dordt spoke definitely of a general, or universal, atonement in the sense of sufficiency. While it is true that the fathers said that Christ's death was "the only and most perfect sacrifice and satisfaction for sin" and was "of infinite worth and value, abundantly sufficient to expiate the sins of the whole world,"[13] the following points must be remembered.

First, this article was included in the Canons to answer the Arminian charge that the Reformed in their doctrine of limited atonement, or particular redemption, do injustice to the sacrifice of Christ and speak disparagingly of its value. That accusation the fathers repudiated. They turned the tables on the Arminians by insisting that not the Reformed but the Arminians spoke disparagingly of the atonement, because they taught that Christ's sacrifice, made for everyone, does not actually save, since many go lost.

Second, the fathers did not intend to teach that actual atonement was made for all men, as is clear from their statement that

---

12 J. I. Packer, "Arminianisms," in *The Manifold Grace of God: Papers Read at the Westminster Conference 1968* (Foxton, England: Burlington Press, 1969), 22–34.

13 Canons of Dordt 2.3, in *Confessions and Church Order,* 163.

"it was the will of God that Christ by the blood of the cross...
should effectually redeem...all those, *and those only,* who were
from eternity chosen to salvation, and given to him by the
Father."[14]

Third, as is plain from Canons 2.3–4, the fathers looked at
sufficiency from the viewpoint of the eternal Son of God, the
one who offered the sacrifice: "This death derives its infinite
value and dignity from these considerations, because the person
who submitted to it was not only really man and perfectly holy,
but also the only begotten Son of God."[15]

Fourth, the intent of Canons 2.3 is merely to state that
because Jesus is the eternal Son of God, his atonement, taken by
itself without any reference to those for whom Christ died, was
of infinite value in God's sight. It was sufficient to expiate the
sins of the whole world because it was God's Son who died; and
God's Son cannot make a sacrifice that, qualitatively speaking, is
a partial sacrifice.

Fifth, it was totally foreign to the thinking of the fathers
at Dordt that Canons 2.3 implied the universal sufficiency of
Christ's death for all men, which the Arminians later claimed.

Another question that needs consideration regarding the
Synod of Dordt deals with the claim of some that the Canons
teach a general offer of the gospel. Those who maintain this
refer especially to the following three articles:

> The promise of the gospel is that whosoever believeth
> in Christ crucified shall not perish, but have everlasting
> life. This promise, together with the command to repent
> and believe, ought to be declared and published to all
> nations, and to all persons promiscuously and without

---

14 Canons of Dordt 2.8, in ibid.; emphasis added.
15 Canons of Dordt 2.4, in ibid.

distinction, to whom God out of his good pleasure sends the gospel.[16]

As many as are called by the gospel are unfeignedly called. For God hath most earnestly and truly shown in his Word what is pleasing to him, namely, that those who are called should come to him. He, moreover, seriously promises eternal life and rest to as many as shall come to him and believe on him.[17]

It is not the fault of the gospel, nor of Christ offered therein, nor of God, who calls men by the gospel and confers upon them various gifts, that those who are called by the ministry of the Word refuse to come and be converted. The fault lies in themselves.[18]

There is no mention in the Canons of the well-meant offer of the gospel in the sense of an intention or desire or will of God, expressed in the gospel, to save all those who hear the gospel. It is true that "offered" is used in Canons 3–4.9, but this word was then commonly used to express the idea that Christ was presented, set forth, or proclaimed in the gospel as the one through whom God accomplished salvation. But that God expresses in the gospel a general desire to save all who hear is an idea totally foreign to the Canons, and it can be read into them only by altering the clear language of the articles and imposing ideas on the fathers of Dordt that they did not have.

Canons 2.5 speaks emphatically of the promise of the gospel and insists that it is particular, that is, only to those who believe in Christ. It is clear from the rest of the Canons that only those

---

16 Canons of Dordt 2.5, in ibid.
17 Canons of Dordt 3–4.8, in ibid., 168.
18 Canons of Dordt 3–4.9, in ibid., 168.

who believe in Christ are the elect, who are converted to God by efficacious grace merited in Christ's particular atonement.[19]

Canons 2.5 also says that the promise ought to be proclaimed everywhere "to whom God out of his good pleasure sends the gospel." So the article speaks clearly of a general proclamation of a particular promise, and this has always been the position held by Reformed churches. This proclamation of the gospel is not heard by all men, but only by those to whom God is pleased to send it.

Canons 2.5 also teaches that this promise, generally proclaimed but particular in its content and address, is declared "together with the command to repent and believe." Canons 3–4.8–9 says that this command is to be the call of the gospel, which is described as being serious. God requires through the preaching that all men forsake their sins, turn from their evil ways, and believe in Christ, who has shed his blood for sin.

No one who stands in the line of Calvinistic and Reformed thought has ever denied this truth. The Reformed have sometimes been charged with being unable to preach the gospel to all men because they insist that the promise of the gospel is for the elect alone. This is a distortion of the Reformed view. The gospel must be generally preached, both because it is the means whereby God calls out of darkness into light those whom he has chosen to everlasting life, and because through this general proclamation all men are confronted with the obligation to forsake their sins and to believe in Christ.

Further, the Reformed have never denied that this command, or call, is serious. God means exactly what he says. He is not joking when he comes to all men with this obligation. He is

---

19 Canons of Dordt 1.6, in ibid., 156: "That some receive the gift of faith from God and others do not receive it proceeds from God's eternal decree."

not saying something in the gospel that is not really true. Quite the opposite is the case. Man was originally created perfect and upright. When man fell in Adam, he fell by his sinful choice. His depravity, which makes it impossible for him to serve God, is his lot in life because of God's just judgment upon sinners.

But God does not on that account require any less of man than he did at the beginning. God is God. He remains just, holy, and righteous in all his ways. He does not say, "Oh, you are a poor sinner who is unable to do what I have commanded; I will not require you to serve me and to flee from your sins. It is perfectly all right if you do less than you were originally required to do." Then God would not be just and righteous. God still insists that man serves him, and man is confronted with this demand every time the gospel comes to him.

Canons 2.5 speaks of the "promise, *together with* the command to repent and believe," as forming the content of the gospel. The command to repent and believe comes to all who hear, including the elect. In this way God works his purpose in his elect by enabling them to repent and believe; and because the command comes to all, the wicked are responsible for their failures to repent and believe. It is not the fault of the gospel, of Christ offered therein, or of God who calls that men refuse to repent. The fault lies in the wicked. So God is perfectly just when he casts the wicked forever from his presence.

If one would object that God is unfair in giving repentance to some and not to others, we answer with Paul, "Nay but, O man, who art thou that repliest against God? Shall the thing formed say to him that formed it, Why hast thou made me thus? Hath not the potter power over the clay, of the same lump to make one vessel unto honour, and another unto dishonour?" (Rom. 9:20–21). Any objection of this sort is a criticism of God's sovereignty and therefore of God himself.

It is easy to see that all this is a far cry from the well-meant offer of the gospel as it is presented and defended today. Of this the fathers at Dordt wanted no part, and to look for support for the well-meant offer in it is a perversion of the Canons.

Even R. B. Kuiper (1886–1966), who was president of Calvin seminary in the 1950s, had difficulty finding confessional grounds for his support of the well-meant offer of the gospel.[20] He could point to only two articles in the Canons. One was Canons 2.5, which cannot in any sense be stretched into supporting a well-meant offer. The other was Canons 2.3, which speaks of the sufficiency of the sacrifice of Christ. Kuiper argued from the statement, "sufficient to expiate the sins of the whole world,"[21] to a position that maintained that Christ's atonement was also *suitable* for all men. From there he argued to the position that the sufficiency and suitability of the atonement were divinely designed for all men. Once again it becomes apparent how the defenders of the well-meant offer of the gospel must make Christ's atonement universal. Kuiper's argument from the Canons was contrived and rationalistic.

Although the offer *per se* was not an issue at Dordt, the Canons do hold to the idea of the general preaching of the gospel, which has always been Reformed, but no appeal to the Canons can support a well-meant offer of the gospel to everyone who hears.

---

20 See chapter 5, "Scriptural Universalism," in R. B. Kuiper, *For Whom Did Christ Die? A Study of the Divine Design of the Atonement* (Grand Rapids, MI: Wm. B. Eerdmans Publishing Company, 1959), 78–100. Kuiper overthrew in chapter 5 everything he had said in the preceding chapters.
21 Canons of Dordt 2.3, in *Confessions and Church Order*, 163.

Chapter 4

AMYRALDISM

Soon after the Synod of Dordt had condemned the Arminian corruptions of sovereign predestination and sovereign grace and had set forth the scriptural teachings concerning these doctrines, the Academy of Saumur in France launched a fierce attack against the Canons. The chief light of the school was Moïse (Moses) Amyraut (1596–1664), who founded what became known as the Amyraldian system of predestination.

The theological school of Saumur was founded by Scotsman John Cameron (1579–1625), Amyraut's teacher. Cameron suggested the lines of thought that Amyraut developed into what became known as hypothetical universalism.

To understand the theological context in which Cameron and Amyraut worked, I note that Cameron and Amyraut claimed that the true teachings of John Calvin, especially on the doctrine of predestination, had been distorted by his successors, notably by Theodore Beza and the theologians of the Synod of Dordt. Cameron and Amyraut were convinced that Beza was mainly responsible for a shift in Calvinism to scholastic theology. That shift to scholastic thought, they said, had distorted Calvin's theology, especially concerning predestination. Cameron and Amyraut, therefore, justified their departures from then-current Calvinistic thought by claiming that they were returning to pristine Calvinism and restoring Calvin's true emphasis, which had been so badly obscured by men who claimed to be followers of Calvin but distorted his central teachings.

Cameron and Amyraut offered as proof for their position that Calvin had not discussed the doctrine of predestination at the beginning of his *Institutes of the Christian Religion* under the heading of the doctrine of God (theology), but had treated it in connection with the doctrine of salvation (soteriology). They claimed that Beza and Dordt moved the treatment of predestination back to theology and therefore made the doctrine speculative. They insisted that predestination belonged to soteriology, where Calvin had placed it, and that soteriology must be treated before predestination to grace as an explanation *ex post facto* of why some believe and others do not. This order makes faith precede predestination.

This view, first proposed by John Cameron, recently has been advanced by others who quarrel with the truth of sovereign predestination and try to make their attacks against this truth sound more reasonable by a reinterpretation of Calvin. However, rarely do they acknowledge that this reinterpretation was first proposed by Amyraut. That it was first proposed by Amyraut certainly casts suspicion on it from the outset.[1]

---

1 Although the Saumur school originated that idea, it has become common in the last half-century to maintain that Calvin's successors distorted his teachings, especially regarding predestination. For an examination of this claim, see Herman Hanko, "The Doctrine of Predestination in Calvin and Beza," *Protestant Reformed Theological Journal* 21, no. 2 (April 1988):24–37; 22, no. 1 (November 1988):29–39; 22, no. 2 (April 1989):3–18; and 23, no. 1 (November 1989):3–19.

There is a *prima facie* case against that interpretation of Calvin, especially regarding Theodore Beza. Calvin and Beza worked together prior to Calvin's death; by Calvin's request Beza was Calvin's successor in the academy in Geneva; and Calvin surely knew Beza's view on predestination and would never have approved of Beza as his successor if Beza diverged so greatly from Calvin's view of the cardinal doctrine of predestination. It is impossible to conceive that Calvin would never have expressed disagreement with Beza's views and would not have protested vehemently Beza's appointment to the academy if Beza was guilty of such great distortion of what Calvin taught. Here is an improbability that no amount of argument can overcome.

While it is true that Calvin developed his views on predestination in connection with soteriology, it is also true that he did not develop them as an *ex post facto* explanation of why some believe and others do not believe. Rather, Calvin taught that predestination is the fountain and cause of faith by which the elect believe and is the divine explanation of why others do not. This is evident from Calvin's teaching concerning predestination in his *Institutes*. Although predestination is developed in connection with soteriology, it is nevertheless mentioned repeatedly throughout the *Institutes*, including in connection with the doctrine of God. Further, Calvin's treatise on predestination and providence, which he wrote in the midst of the Bolsec controversy, shows decisively the error of Cameron's and Amyraut's view. Historically, then, their position is untenable.

The motivation behind the teaching of Cameron and Amyraut was to prove their claim that Calvin's doctrine of predestination had been distorted. Cameron claimed to proceed from a covenantal position. He taught that God established a twofold covenant: one an absolute covenant, unconditional and rooted in antecedent love; the other a hypothetical covenant, dependent on man's fulfillment of the condition of love. He said that the hypothetical covenant was the important one, because it was the covenant of experience. However, the power of man's love is always God's antecedent love.

On the basis of that same distinction Amyraut developed hypothetical universalism. He followed Cameron's views of the covenant and agreed that the hypothetical covenant was the important one, because it is the covenant of revelation and experience. Within this covenant the essential elements are obligation and promised reward, the latter conditioned by the former.

Amyraut taught that an important distinction must be made between the Mosaic covenant, which is legal, and the gracious covenant, which is of promise. Amyraut said that all mankind are the contracting parties of the gracious covenant, the condition for the fulfillment of the covenant is faith, the promise is eternal life, the mediator is Christ, and the efficacy is God's work of mercy. As one traces Amyraut's views, he becomes increasingly convinced that the more recent views of a conditional covenant originated with Amyraut's covenantal approach.

Amyraut's views of predestination followed from his idea of the covenant. He developed those views especially in his brief treatise on predestination, written fifteen years after the Synod of Dordt had adjourned.[2] In this treatise Amyraut developed his idea of two wills in God: a particular and unconditional will and a universal and conditional will. These two wills, Amyraut said, are irreconcilable and part of the hidden mystery of God's decree.[3]

---

2   Moïse Amyraut, *Brief traitte de la predestination et des ses principales dependances* [Brief treatise on predestination and its dependent principles] (Saumur: Jean Lesnier & Isaac Desbordes, 1634).

3   Moïse Amyraut, *Brief Treatise on Predestination and Its Dependent Principles,* trans. Richard Lum ([United States]: n.p., 1985), 38–44, 51–58. See also Brian G. Armstrong, *Calvinism and the Amyraut Heresy: Protestant*

The double-will idea, Amyraut claimed, had been taught by Calvin and was fundamental to Calvin's teaching. It is true that Calvin distinguished between the will of God's decree and the will of God's precept (his revealed will), but Calvin specifically repudiated the idea that these were separate wills that contradicted each other—something Amyraut insisted was true. Calvin said that God has one will in which his decree and his command are in perfect harmony with each other.

On the basis of the distinction between God's particular will and God's universal will, Amyraut taught that universal and conditional predestination is a part of providence. It is a part of two counsels in God that he prepared because of the fall. According to his universal and conditional will, God wills the salvation of all men and promises salvation to all on the condition of faith. Only because God knows that man is incapable of believing, God also particularly and unconditionally wills to save the elect.

Amyraut admitted that he emphasized Calvin's "double-will" idea more than Calvin did, but that was necessary because scholastic theologians repudiated it, and he could restore the true balance of pure Calvinism only by emphasizing what was being so sorely neglected. Amyraut wrote,

> These words, "God desires the salvation of all men," (1 Tim. 2:4) receive this necessary limitation, "providing that they believe." If they do not believe, he does not desire it. This will to make the grace of salvation universal and common to all men is in this way conditional, that without the accomplishing of the condition, it is entirely ineffectual.[4]

Scholasticism and Humanism in Seventeenth-Century France (Madison, WI: University of Wisconsin Press, 1969), 158–221.

4   Amyraut, *Brief Treatise on Predestination*, 43.

Amyraut also wrote, "God wills all men to be saved...He invites them to repent...He extends His arms to them...He goes before them and calls them with a lively voice."[5]

Here is the essence of the well-meant offer of the gospel as proposed by Amyraut. The essential idea of the well-meant offer is that God desires the salvation of all men without exception, or if that is too broad, God desires the salvation of all who hear the gospel, and he expresses that desire in the gospel. Amyraut proposed exactly that idea with his hypothetical universalism.

The proponents of the well-meant offer of the gospel are unclear on this point. If the gospel is the means whereby God expresses his desire to save, then only those who hear the gospel are the objects of God's desire and intention. However, others consistently insist that God's will is to save all men, which means that God seeks the salvation of all men, whether they hear the gospel or not. Because it is important that men know this, some seem to suggest that God's desire to save those who never hear the gospel is expressed in an attitude of favor, which is supposed to be made known in the creation, such as by rain and sunshine.

Hence, because the gospel expresses God's universal will to save all men, it comes to men as an *offer* to all. At the Synod of Alençon, before which Amyraut was called to appear and answer for his views, he said,

> So that those who are called by the Preaching of the Gospel to participate by Faith in the Effects and Fruits of his Death, being invited seriously, and God vouchsafing them all external Means needful for their coming to him, and showing them in good earnest, and with the greatest Sincerity by his Word, what would be

---

5   Moïse Amyraut, *Six Sermons of 1636*, quoted in Armstrong, *Calvinism and the Amyraut Heresy*, 184.

well-pleasing to him, if they should not believe in the Lord Jesus Christ, but perish in their Obstinacy and Unbelief; this cometh not from any Defect of Virtue or Sufficiency in the Sacrifice of Jesus Christ, nor yet for want of Summons or serious Invitations unto Faith or Repentance, but only from their own Fault.[6]

The external call of the gospel, according to Amyraut, speaks of a sufficiency of salvation for all, a universal will of God to save all, and an objective grace for all that is needful for their coming to Christ. The subjective grace of salvation is dependent and conditioned on faith. The objective grace is an offer of pardon to all, while the subjective grace, or salvation, is conditional and only for those who come to Christ. These two graces correspond to the double will of God. The universal grace objectively given corresponds to God's universal will to save all, while the subjective grace flows from God's particular will to save only the elect.

All of this is rooted in the atonement, which is universal in sufficiency, intention, and scope. The atonement merits grace that is objectively for all but is subjectively given only to those who fulfill the condition of faith.

Francis Turretin quoted Testardus, a disciple of Amyraut.

The end of giving Christ for a propitiation in his blood was, that a new covenant might be entered into with the whole human family, and that without any impeachment of justice, their salvation might be rendered possible, and an offer of it made to them in the gospel.

---

6   Armstrong, *Calvinism and the Amyraut Heresy*, 93. Armstrong quoted from John Quick, *Synodicon in Gallia Reformata: or, the Acts, Decisions, Decrees, and Canons of Those Famous National Councils of the Reformed Churches in France* (London: n.p., 1692), 2:354.

In this sense, indeed, no one who believes the word of God, can deny that Christ died for all men.[7]

Turretin quoted from chapter 7 of Amyraut's *Brief Treatise on Predestination.*

Since the misery of the human family is equal and universal, and the desire which God has to free them from it by a Redeemer, proceeds from the mercy which he exercises towards us as his creatures fallen into destruction, in which we are all equal; the grace of redemption, that he has procured for us, and offers us, should be equal and universal, provided we are equally disposed to its reception.[8]

At the heart of Amyraut's views was his conception of a double will of God. That view was then and is now closely linked with the well-meant offer of the gospel. It is easy to see why this is true. Those who maintain a well-meant offer teach that God desires the salvation of all who hear the gospel and God expresses his desire in the preaching of the gospel. Thus they conclude that God wills the salvation of everyone who hears the gospel. However, if one wants to maintain a semblance of being Reformed and Calvinistic, one must also insist that according to the decree of election, God wills to save only some. The only way to include both ideas in one system of theology is to posit an irreconcilable contradiction within the will of God: God wills that all men be saved, and God wills that only some be saved.

---

7   James R. Willson, *A Historical Sketch of Opinions on the Atonement: Interspersed with Biographical Notices of the Leading Doctors, and Outlines of the Sections of the Church, from the Incarnation of Christ to the Present Time, with Translations from Francis Turrettin on the Atonement* (Philadelphia: Edward Earle, 1817), 292.

8   Ibid., 293.

It will not do to appeal to Calvin as if he taught a double will of God, because it has been proven that he did not. While Calvin distinguished within the will of God, he found perfect harmony and unity between the two aspects of God's will, and he denied that God in any sense wills the salvation of all men.

Although earlier in the history of the reformers and of Dordt, certain ideas closely related to the well-meant offer were brought up, Amyraut was the first to set forth a clearly worked out conception of the well-meant offer of the gospel. The defenders of the offer ought to take note of this. Their doctrine does not stand in the line of Reformed thinking through Dordt; it owes its origin to Amyraldism and the heresy of the theologians of Saumur.

Inseparably connected with the well-meant offer is universal atonement. Dordt spoke of a certain infinite value to the sacrifice of Christ, but the Saumur theologians went beyond that and taught universality as to sufficiency, intention, and scope. They limited the efficacy of the atonement to the elect, although they made efficacy to be conditioned on faith. The connection between the universality of the command and the well-meant offer is clear. If God offers salvation to everyone in a serious and well-meaning way, it follows that salvation must somehow be rooted in the cross. That can only mean that in some sense the atonement is universal, since God cannot offer what is not available.

Without discussing at length hypothetical universalism as taught by the Saumur theologians, it ought to be noted that a defense of the well-meant offer of the gospel inevitably involves one in a denial of the truth of sovereign predestination. The two may perhaps be maintained side by side in some unhappy, contradictory way for a time, but the inevitable consequence is that sooner or later both contradictory ideas cannot be maintained, and predestination always falls by the way. That was true of the school of Saumur, and it is equally true today. No wonder. How can one maintain the doctrine of sovereign predestination when he believes in a double-will theory? How can one consistently and clearly maintain God's sovereign choice of his people and his sovereign damnation of the wicked in the way of their sins when he believes that God wills the salvation of all men according to his revealed will? This is utterly impossible.

Amyraut taught universal objective grace and particular subjective grace, both merited in the cross. While he did not call universal objective grace "common," his idea of objective grace was strikingly similar to what in more recent times is known as common grace. Throughout church history the well-meant offer has more often than not been connected with common grace. This ought not to surprise us. If God sincerely wills the salvation of all men, or at least of everyone who hears the gospel, then through the gospel God shows his favor, love, grace, and mercy to everyone who hears the gospel and not only to his people. It ought to give the defenders of common grace pause that both ideas have their origin in Amyraldism. More modern defenders of the well-meant offer go farther than Amyraut and teach that God gives subjective grace as well to everyone who hears the gospel.

Perhaps the defenders of the well-meant offer of the gospel are not concerned about being Amyraldian, but they must admit that they stand outside the line of the Reformation and Dordt and stand squarely in the tradition of Amyraut and his opposition to the decisions of the Synod of Dordt.

Amyraut's conception necessitated the teaching of conditional salvation. The revealed covenant, according to Amyraut, is conditional; the revealed will of God to save all men is conditional; the offer of salvation is conditional; and the promise of Christ is conditional—in every case the condition is faith. This connection between conditional theology and the well-meant offer is also an idea that should not surprise us. Conditional theology has always been inseparably related to the well-meant offer and is an integral part of a conception that presents God as willing the salvation of all men. This is easy to understand. If God wills the salvation of all men, why are only some saved? The answer given to that question is, only those who believe are saved. Salvation, then, is conditioned on faith and given only after the exercise of faith.

Conditional salvation is an Arminian concept. One might object to a charge of Arminianism by saying that Amyraut, and those who try to maintain conditional salvation, insisted that God gives grace to fulfill the condition. While salvation is prepared for all men, offered to all, and willed for all, it is dependent on faith for its realization in the hearts of those who accept Christ. But faith, so it is claimed, is actually worked by God, and in this way the sovereignty and efficacy of grace is said to be maintained.

It is nonsense to say that Christ died (in some real sense) for everyone, and that his cross is efficacious, but that only some are actually saved because its efficacy is limited to some. It is nonsense to say that God entreats everyone to be saved as his most earnest will, but he promises salvation only to those who believe, when God is the giver of faith.

Is faith part of salvation, or is faith a condition to salvation? It cannot be both. If faith is a condition to salvation, it is not part of salvation. If faith is not part of salvation, it is not worked by God. To maintain both at the same time is patent nonsense and impossible for any intelligent person to believe.

Is election conditioned on faith, as the Arminians teach? If it is, election cannot be the fountain and cause of faith, as scripture teaches, for it cannot be both the condition to election and the fruit of election.

Is faith part of the promise proclaimed in the gospel, or is faith a condition to the promise? That is, when God through the gospel promises salvation, does he promise it to everyone conditioned on faith? Then faith is not part of the promise of salvation but is a condition to it, and faith is man's work. Conditional salvation and a general offer go hand in hand. They are both Arminian and Amyraldian.

The Reformed and Calvinistic doctrine is that faith is part of the promise of salvation, one of the gifts of salvation—of a salvation that is promised only to the elect, proclaimed through the gospel, and worked by God in the hearts of those for whom Christ died.

Pierre du Moulin (1568–1658), a Frenchman who taught for a short time in the University of Leiden, was a strong opponent of Arminianism, Amyraldism, and the concept of the well-meant offer of the gospel. Du Moulin also served in the prestigious church of Charenton, just outside Paris. He was appointed as a delegate to the Synod of Dordt, but the French government forbade him to attend.

Du Moulin wrote the following:

> If any doctrine be contumelious [stubbornly perverse or rebellious] against God, this is, accusing him of folly, putting upon him human affections, and falsely attributing to him wishes of no strength, and a desire of no force: as if they should bring in God speaking thus: I do indeed earnestly desire to save you, but ye hinder, that I cannot do what I desire; I would if you would: therefore seeing by you I am frustrated of my intent, I will change my purpose of saving you, and my will being otherwise bent, I have determined to destroy you for ever. It is certainly plain, that this antecedent will of God, is not a

will; but a desire and wish, which God doth obtain only by entreaty.

Furthermore, how grievous a thing it is to be defrauded of one's desire and natural affection, and how disagreeing this is to God, who doth not see, unless it be he that will willingly be deceived? For if God be most perfectly good, yea goodness itself, it must needs be, that his affections and natural desires (if he have any) are of highest sanctity, justice, and perfection: and therefore nothing is so much to be wished, as that that natural affection might be fulfilled, and that God might obtain his desired end. There is cause therefore that we should grieve for God's cause, who is deceived of that end which is far the best and who might be made partaker of his wish, if man would let him. See whether the wit of these innovators doth plunge itself, and how honourably they think of God...

If God from eternity knows that this man shall be damned, in vain doth he wish from eternity, that he should be saved: and he doth from eternity know that he shall not be partaker of his natural desire, and his antecedent will...

What a thing is it, that hereby there is brought in resistance between these two wills of God, the latter of which doth correct the former, for by this antecedent will, God doth desire to do that, which from eternity he is certain he shall not do. And God is imagined doing something hardly and unwillingly, and against that end which he had first intended, because man's will comes between, by which it comes to pass, that God doth cease from that end propounded to himself, which was far better, as if per *deutopon ploun*, upon a second advice, he should obtain some secondary good. Arminius doth not dissemble this, whole words are these: God doth seriously desire all men should be saved, but being compelled by the stubborn and incorrigible malice of some men he will have them make loss of their salvation. But God doth nothing unwillingly, neither can he be compelled by man, to the changing of his will...

To which purpose, excellently Saint Augustine [states in] *Enchiridion,* Chapter 95, "Our God in heaven doth whatsoever things he will, both in heaven and earth; which is not true, if he hath willed some things, and hath not done them: And which is more unworthy of him, hath not therefore done them, because the will of man hath hindered that the Almighty should not do what he willed." [9]

Du Moulin wrote further:

By the way, the reader shall observe, that unproper phrases, and spoken after the manner of men, ought not to be taken as properly spoken. God is figuratively said to have wished and expected fruit from his vine. Desires, and grief, as if having spent his labour in vain he had failed of his propounded end, cannot happen to God.[10]

---

9   Pierre du Moulin, *The Anatomy of Arminianisme: or The Opening of the Controuersies Lately Handled in the Low-Countryes: concerning the Doctrine of Prouidence, of Predestination, of the Death of Christ, of Nature and Grace* (London: T[homas] S[nowdam] for Nathaniel Newbery, 1620), 29–33. Quotations from this book with modernized spelling were accessed at http://www.cprf.co.uk, the website of the Covenant Protestant Reformed Church in Northern Ireland.

10 Ibid., 480–81.

In explanations of the texts appealed to by defenders of the well-meant offer, Moulin wrote the following:

[Matthew 23:37] signifieth quite another thing [than Arminius supposes]. Christ speaks to Jerusalem, and saith, that he would have gathered his children together; but Jerusalem herself resisted, with all her power. Jerusalem is one thing, and her children another, who here are expressly distinguished from the city: By Jerusalem understood the priests, the Levites, the scribes, and the prince of the people, for these did most of all withstand Christ: By the children of Jerusalem, understand the people. Christ saith, that he would have gathered together these children; neither is it to be doubted, but that he gathered together many of them although the rulers were unwilling...Saint [Augustine] thinks [*Enchiridion*, chapter 97]...she indeed would not have her children to be gathered together by him: but even [though] she [was] unwilling, he gathered those of her children whom he himself would.[11]

They [the Arminians] do colourably boast of that place, 1 Tim. 2:4 *God would have all men to be saved, and come to the knowledge of the truth.* And verse 6, *Christ gave himself a ransom for all.* Also that to Titus, chap. 2 *The grace of God, that bringeth salvation unto all men, hath appeared*: But that here, by *all*, are understood *any*, and men, of whatsoever state and condition, the very context and coherence of the place doth prove. In that place to Timothy, the apostle would have kings to be prayed for; in that place to Titus, he commandeth servants to

---

11 Ibid., 36–37; see also 479.

be faithful, and not to purloin. Of this exhortation, this is the cause and reason; because the promise of salvation did belong to kings, although at that time they were strangers from Christ; and to servants, although they were of an abject and base state; neither is any condition of men excluded from salvation. Saint [Augustine] doth thus take this place of the first [letter] to Timothy [*Enchiridion*, chapter 103]. And [so too does] Thomas [Aquinas] in his commentary upon this epistle...For if God should absolutely will, or should seriously desire all and particular men to be saved, there would not be wanting means to him, whereby he might effect what he would, and [they] be made partakers of his desire.[12]

God saith in these words; *I am not delighted with the death of a sinner, but that he should be converted, and live* [Ezek. 18:23]. These words [contrary to the Arminians] say nothing else than that God will[s] not the death of that sinner who is converted: But if he be not converted, Arminius himself will not deny, but that God doth will his death; as the judge doth will the punishment of him that is guilty. God is not delighted with the death of a sinner, as he is a man, but yet no man can deny, but that God loveth the execution of his justice.[13]

Francis Turretin (1623–87), a contemporary of Amyraut, taught in Geneva while the Amyraldian controversy raged in France. In part as a response to the heresy of Amyraldism, Turretin helped write the Formula Consensus Helvetica (1675).[14] A

---

12 Ibid., 247–49; see also 355.
13 Ibid., 250.
14 Formula Consensus Helvetica, composed at Zurich in 1675 by John Henry Heidegger, of Zurich, assisted by Francis Turretine, of Geneva, and Luke

few articles in the Consensus were specifically written against the Amyraldian heresy, and they repudiate the well-meant offer of the gospel. While this confession never received confessional status in the Presbyterian and Reformed churches, it nevertheless indicates how Turretin opposed what Amyraut taught.

Article 13 of the Consensus emphatically sets forth the unconditionality of the covenant and the particularity of Christ's atoning sacrifice.

> As Christ was from eternity elected the Head, Prince, and Lord (*Hœres*) of all who, in time, are saved by His grace, so also, in time, He was made Surety of the New Covenant only for those who, by the eternal Election, were given to Him as His own people (*populus peculii*), His seed and inheritance. For according to the determinate counsel of the Father and His own intention, He encountered dreadful death instead of the elect alone, restored only these into the bosom of the Father's grace, and these only He reconciled to God, the offended Father, and delivered from the curse of the law. For our Jesus saves *His people* from their sins (Matt. 1:21), who gave His life a ransom for *many sheep* (Matt. 20:28; John 10:15), His own, who hear His voice (John 10:27–28), and for those only He also intercedes, as a divinely appointed Priest, and not for the world (John 17:9). Accordingly in the death of Christ, only the elect, who in time are made new creatures (2 Cor. 5:17), and for whom Christ in

Gernler, of Basle, and designed to condemn and exclude that modified form of Calvinism, which, in the seventeenth century, emanated from the theological school at Saumur, represented by Amyraut, Josua Placeus, and Jean Daille. The Formula is quoted in appendix 2 in Archibald Alexander Hodge, *Outlines of Theology* (New York: Robert Carter and Brothers, 1878), 656–63.

His death was substituted as an expiatory sacrifice, are regarded as having died with Him and as being justified from sin; and thus, with the counsel of the Father who gave to Christ none but the elect to be redeemed, and also with the working of the Holy Spirit, who sanctifies and seals unto a living hope of eternal life none but the elect, the will of Christ who died so agrees and amicably conspires in perfect harmony, that the sphere of the Father's election (*Patris eligentis*), the Son's redemption (*Filii redimentis*), and the Spirit's sanctification (*Spiritus S. sanctificantus*) is one and the same (œqualis *pateat*).[15]

Article 16 specifically condemns Amyraut's errors but does not mention his name.

Since all these things are entirely so, surely we can not approve the contrary doctrine of those who affirm that of His own intention, by His own counsel and that of the Father who sent Him, Christ died for all and each upon the impossible condition, provided they believe; that He obtained for all a salvation, which, nevertheless, is not applied to all, and by His death merited salvation and faith for no one individually and certainly *(proprie et actu)*, but only removed the obstacle of Divine justice, and acquired for the Father the liberty of entering into a new covenant of grace with all men; and finally, they so separate the active and passive righteousness of Christ, as to assert that He claims His *active* righteousness for himself as His own, but gives and imputes only His *passive* righteousness to the elect. All these opinions, and all that are like these, are contrary to the plain

---

15 Formula Consensus Helvetica 13, in ibid., 659.

Scriptures and the glory of Christ, who is *Author and Finisher* of our faith and salvation; they make His cross of none effect, and under the appearance of augmenting His merit, they really diminish it.[16]

Article 19 addresses the subject of the call of the gospel.

Moreover, because God approved every verity which flows from His counsel, therefore it is rightly said to be His will, that *all who see the Son and believe on Him may have everlasting life* (John 6:40). Although these "all" are the elect alone, and God formed no plan of universal salvation without any selection of persons, and Christ therefore died not for every one but for the elect only who were given to Him.[17]

The command of the gospel spoken of in the Formula and directed to everyone who hears the gospel must be distinguished clearly from the well-meant offer. Sometimes Reformed theologians used *offer* in the sense of a command. Nevertheless, the idea of a command must be distinguished from what is commonly taught by those who maintain the well-meant offer. They teach that through the preaching God expresses his desire, willingness, and intention to save everyone who hears the gospel, because it is his revealed will to save all men, and his revealed will is rooted in some sense in an atonement for all men.

The biblical and confessional view is that through the preaching of the gospel, the *command* to repent of sin and to believe is an entirely different idea than God's desire to save everyone who hears the preaching. This command to repent and believe is rooted in the creation ordinance. God created man

16 Formula Consensus Helvetica 16, in ibid., 660.
17 Formula Consensus Helvetica 19, in ibid., 661.

good and upright, capable in all things of willing the will of God. When man fell he lost all ability to obey God and to keep his commandments; man plunged himself into the ruin of sin and death. However, God does not withdraw his requirement that man must obey him because man, through his foolishness, lost the ability to love and serve God. God is just and righteous in everything he does. Whether man can or cannot keep God's law makes no difference; God still requires of man what he originally required when he created man upright and able to serve him.

Here too Arminianism and Calvinism part ways. Arminianism takes the position that obligation can rest only upon ability. This is dangerously false and utterly contrary to scripture. The Heidelberg Catechism (1563) puts a stop to such evil thinking when it says in question and answer 9:

> Q. Doth not God then do injustice to man, by requiring from him in his law that which he can not perform?
>
> A. Not at all; for God made man capable of performing it; but man, by the instigation of the devil, and his own willful disobedience, deprived himself and all his posterity of those divine gifts.[18]

This truth forms the basis for the command to everyone who hears the gospel to turn from sin and obey God.

Turretin struggled with the question of how the command to believe in Christ can come to all men when Christ did not die for all men. To solve that problem, Turretin distinguished between the direct act of faith and the reflex act of faith, the former referring only to the command to believe in Christ as one in whom is full salvation for those who come to him, and the

---

18 Heidelberg Catechism, Q&A 9, in *Confessions and Church Order*, 86–87.

latter being the act of faith whereby one personally appropriates Christ as one's own. Only the former is the content of the command that comes to everyone who hears the gospel.

Is Turretin's distinction satisfactory? The scriptures do not speak of such a distinction in faith when they make clear that all men who hear the gospel must be confronted with the command to believe. However, Turretin looked at the matter from the viewpoint of the one to whom the command comes. Although it is true that the command to believe in Christ includes the command to assent to the scriptures as true and to believe that Christ's sacrifice is the perfect and complete sacrifice for sin, it is clear that with his distinction Turretin separated assent from assurance as faith chronologically operates in the believer. It is the same distinction that arose in later discussions in Reformed and Presbyterian theology between the assurance of faith and the essence of faith. It suggests a historical faith, which is only assent to truth and is not a personal assurance that Christ died for me.

This is unsatisfactory, for to believe that Christ's sacrifice is the perfect and complete sacrifice for sin necessarily implies a personal fleeing from sin and a resting in Christ, that is, a personal appropriation that Christ is indeed one's savior and redeemer. The command to believe in Christ is not a bare command to believe that God's work of the sacrifice of Christ for sin is true without a personal commitment to that truth. Added to the command to believe in Christ must be the promise of the gospel that whoever believes will be saved. No one can believe that Christ died for sin without believing that Christ died for him who believes.

Chapter 5

—⟨⟩—

THE WESTMINSTER ASSEMBLY

The error of Amyraldism was not confined to France but soon spread to many parts of the continent and to Britain. It appeared especially in the teachings of John Davenant (1576–1641), whom many consider to be one of Britain's outstanding theologians. He was one of the delegates from Great Britain to the Synod of Dordt.

Davenant attempted to find a middle road between outright Arminianism and the supralapsarianism that some in England favored. He found in the theology of Saumur such a road, and he defended the Amyraldian views of hypothetical universalism, general atonement in the sense of intention and sufficiency to save all men, a universal blessing of the cross, and conditional salvation. While Davenant may not have accepted everything Amyraut taught, Davenant was sympathetic to Amyraut's general position on the extent of the atonement.

The British delegation to the Synod of Dordt regularly sent letters to Dudley Carleton, ambassador to the Netherlands. The letters, written by John Hales, the ambassador's chaplain, and

CORRUPTING THE WORD OF GOD

Walter Balcanqual, contained the reactions of the British delegation to the synod.[1]

One letter, signed by John Davenant, described his views on the extent of Christ's atonement.

According to these two last Propositions we do hold, "that our Blessed Saviour by God's Appointment did offer up himself to the *Blessed Trinity* for the *Redemption of man*kind, and by this oblation once made, did found, confirm, and ratifie the *Evangelical Covenant*, which may and ought to be preached seriously to all mankind without exception…And moreover we hold this ensuing Proposition, which we also have exhibited, and which was in like sort approved by the rest…

And according to this we hold, that there are sundry initial preparations tending to Conversion, merited by Christ, and dispensed in the preaching of the Gospel, and wrought by the Holy Ghost in the hearts of many that never attain to true Regeneration or Justification.[2]

Many in England were highly critical of the Synod of Dordt for two reasons. First, the British delegates claimed that the synod and especially the president, Johannes Bogerman, were too harsh with the Arminians and treated them in an

---

1 "Mr. Hales Letters from the Synod of Dort to the Right Honourable Sir Dudley Carlton, Lord Ambassador, Etc.," in John M. Hales, *Golden Remains of the Ever Memorable Mr. John Hales of Eton College*, John Pearson, ed. (London: Printed for Timothy Garthwait, at the Little Northdoor of St. Pauls, 1659), 1–80; and "Dr. Balcanquals Letters from the Synod of Dort to the Right Honourable Sir Dudley Carlton, Lord Ambassador, Etc.," in ibid., 1–37.

2 Anthony Milton, ed., *The British Delegation and the Synod of Dort (1618–1619)*, Church of England Record Society (Woodridge, UK: The Boydell Press, 2005), 13:219.

un-Christian way, especially by their abrupt dismissal of them. Second, the Canons are far too rigid in their defense of the faith and radical in the extreme in their doctrinal pronouncements. The publication of the letters describing the synod was fuel for their fire, and they published them eagerly and enthusiastically.

The views of Davenant were closely connected with the theology of the well-meant offer of salvation to all men. It is clear that he defended a view that was contrary to the views of Calvin, and Davenant attempted to alter the system of Calvinism as it was maintained by many theologians within Britain.

Paul Helm discussed Davenant's views and quoted him in a book he wrote to refute Dr. R. T. Kendall, who defended the proposition that Puritan theology departed significantly from, and even opposed, the theology of John Calvin, especially his doctrine of the atonement.

> According to Kendall, Calvin held that the scope of the death of Christ is different from that of his intercession. He died for all, but intercedes only for the elect. The Amyraldians appear to have made no such distinction, arguing that the work of Christ *as a totality* was for all, and that this total saving work was applied by the Holy Spirit to the elect alone. According to Kendall's Calvin, only part of the provision of salvation in Christ was universal in its intent, namely, his death, while his intercession was particular. It is this that makes his interpretation of Calvin unique.
>
> In his *Dissertation on the Death of Christ*, a book written from a broadly Amyraldian position, John Davenant considers the following objection to his own view:
>
>> If the death of Christ is to be considered as a remedy or ransom applicable to every man, from the

ordination of God, then also the resurrection, intercession and mediation of Christ will have respect to all men in the same manner. But Christ was not raised up for all men, does not intercede for all, is not the mediator of all: Therefore, neither is his death to be extended to all.

It might be expected that Davenant would reply to such an objection by insisting that the scope of Christ's intercession is narrower than that of his death, and by backing that up with an appeal to the illustrious precedent of John Calvin. But Davenant replies,

For as we can truly announce to every man that his sins are expiable by the death of Christ according to the ordination of God, and will be expiated, if only he should believe in Christ; so also we can truly declare, that the same Christ was raised again, that he might justify him through faith, and was exalted at the right hand of God, that, by his mediation and merits, he might preserve him through faith in the favour of God, and at length might lead him to glory. Therefore we do not put asunder those things which God hath joined together; but we teach that the death, resurrection, and intercession of Christ are joined together in indissoluble union.[3]

It is clear from this quotation that Davenant wanted universal atonement in some respects and an intercession of Christ that had the same extent as the atonement.

---

3   Paul Helm, *Calvin and the Calvinists* (Edinburgh: Banner of Truth Trust, 1982), 36–37.

A similar assessment of Davenant's position was taken in a paper entitled "Universalism and the Reformed Churches."

> In England the notion of a universal desire in God for the salvation of all men was also the root principle of the Davenant School at the beginning of the seventeenth century. This school taught that there is in the redemption purchased by Christ, an absolute intention for the elect and a conditional intention for the reprobate in case they do not believe.[4]

Davenant influenced some men, and his school of thought was represented at the Westminster Assembly. Those men generally agreed in an absolute decree of predestination for the elect and in a general and conditional decree for all men. They defended universal atonement in God's intention and in its sufficiency. Flowing from the cross are general blessings for all men, and a certain common grace is the possession of all who come under the preaching. Those men also defended the offer of the gospel to all men in which God expressed his intention and willingness to save all.

A. F. Mitchell wrote concerning the Westminster Confession:

> The same care was taken to avoid the insertion of anything which could be regarded as indicating a preference for *supralapsarianism;* and for this purpose, the words, "to bring this to pass, God ordained to permit man to

---

4 Evangelical Presbyterian Church of Australia, *Universalism and the Reformed Churches: A Defense of Calvin's Calvinism* (Launceston, Tasmania: Magazine and Literature Committee of the Evangelical Presbyterian Church of Australia, repr., 1997), 5. This paper is a detailed refutation of the idea that the well-meant offer of the gospel stands in the line of historic Calvinism. It clearly shows that the well-meant offer is a modification of Calvinism that introduces deadly Arminianism into the Calvinistic system.

fall," were changed into "they who are elected, being fallen in Adam, are redeemed by Christ," etc. Did these divines mean to follow an opposite policy in regard to the point on which Calamy, Arrowsmith, Vines, Seaman, and other disciples of Davenant, or according to Baillie of Amyraut, differed from the more exact Calvinists? After repeated perusal of their debate, I cannot take upon myself certainly to affirm that they did, though I admit that this matter is not so clear as the others above referred to. No notes of the debate in its latest stage are given, nor is any vote of dissent respecting it found in these Minutes. Calamy, who spoke repeatedly in the debate on the Extent of Redemption, avowed that he held, in the same sense as the English divines at the Synod of Dort, "that Christ by his death did pay a price for all, with absolute intention for the elect, with conditional intention for the reprobate in case they do believe; that all men should be *salvabiles non obstante lapsu Adami*; that Jesus Christ did not only die sufficiently for all, but God did intend, in giving of Christ, and Christ in giving himself did intend, to put all men in a state of salvation in case they do believe." Seaman, Vines, Marshall, and Harris, in part at least, agreed with him. And though I cannot find that Dr. Arrowsmith took part in this debate, yet he was attending the Assembly, was a member of the Committee on the Confession, and in his writings has repeatedly expressed his leaning toward the same opinion.[5]

---

5 Alex F. Mitchell, introduction, in Alex F. Mitchell and John Struthers, eds., *Minutes of the Sessions of the Westminster Assembly of Divines* (Edinburgh: William Blackwood & Sons, 1874), lv–lvi. The men whom Mitchell

In this same connection Philip Schaff wrote,

Several prominent members [of the Westminster Assembly], as Calamy, Arrowsmith, Vines, Seaman, who took part in the preparation of the doctrinal standards, sympathized with the hypothetical universalism of the Saumur school (Cameron and Amyrauld) and with the moderate position of Davenant and the English delegates to the Synod of Dort. They expressed this sympathy on the floor of the Assembly, as well as on other occasions. They believed in a special *effective* election and final perseverance of the elect (as necessary means to a certain end), but they held at the same time that God sincerely *intends* to save *all* men; that Christ *intended* to die, and *actually* died, for *all* men; and that the difference is not in the intention and offer on the part of God, but in the acceptance and appropriation on the part of men.[6]

Were those views of the Davenant school incorporated into the Westminster Confession (1647)? The answer is that although able theologians defended those views at the assembly, they were not included in the formulation of the Westminster Confession as it was finally adopted. The following article does not mention the hypothetical universalism of the Saumur school and emphatically sets forth sovereign and double predestination:

The rest of mankind God was pleased, according to the unsearchable counsel of his own will, whereby he extendeth or withholdeth mercy, as he pleaseth, for the glory

---

mentions held to Amyraldian views, which is clear from the record of the *Minutes* (152–56).

6 Schaff, *Creeds of Christendom*, 1:770.

of his sovereign power over his creatures, to pass by, and to ordain them to dishonor and wrath for their sin, to the praise of his glorious justice.[7]

In connection with the redemption Christ accomplished on the cross, the Westminster Assembly was equally strong.

The Lord Jesus, by his perfect obedience and sacrifice of himself, which he through the eternal Spirit once offered up unto God,...purchased...an everlasting inheritance in the kingdom of heaven for all those whom the Father hath given unto him.[8]

Although the work of redemption was not actually wrought by Christ till after his incarnation, yet the virtue, efficacy, and benefits thereof were communicated unto the elect.[9]

To all those for whom Christ hath purchased redemption he doth certainly and effectually apply and communicate the same.[10]

Yet the above articles do not entirely solve the problem, for the much-debated question is, did the Westminster divines specifically and categorically exclude the Amyraldian view as set forth by the Davenant school?

The Westminster Confession specifically referred to the offer in 7.3, where it unexpectedly appears in connection with the doctrine of the covenant rather than where one would expect it in connection with the calling.

---

7   Westminster Confession of Faith 3.7, in ibid., 3:610.
8   Westminster Confession of Faith 8.5, in ibid., 3:621.
9   Westminster Confession of Faith 8.6, in ibid.
10 Westminster Confession of Faith 8.8, in ibid., 3:622.

Man by his fall having made himself incapable of life by that covenant, the Lord was pleased to make a second, commonly called the covenant of grace: wherein he freely offered unto sinners life and salvation by Jesus Christ, requiring of them faith in him that they may be saved, and promising to give unto all those that are ordained unto life his Holy Spirit, to make them willing and able to believe.[11]

Although "offered" is used in the above article,[12] there are several considerations that lead to a conclusion that the Westminster divines did not use "offered" as the Saumur school and the Davenant men had used and intended it. The Westminster divines did not incorporate into the creed the theology of the offer—a double will of God, a universal intention in the atonement, and conditional salvation. The word *offer* is not found in the chapter on effectual calling, where one would expect it, but it is found in the section on the covenant, which leads one to think that the Westminster divines intended it in the sense of Christ *presented*, or *set forth*, in the gospel. Even where "offered" is used in 7.3, it is synonymous with the command to believe: "freely offered unto sinners life and salvation by Jesus Christ, *requiring* of them faith in him." The article says that the promise of salvation is to the elect alone: "and promising to give unto all those that are ordained unto life his Holy Spirit, to make them willing and able to believe."[13]

Nevertheless, the views represented at the Westminster Assembly by the Davenant men were not specifically repudiated. Some have argued from this that the assembly deliberately worded the Westminster Confession in such a way that the

---

11 Westminster Confession of Faith 7.3, in ibid., 3:617.
12 Latin: *in quo peccatoribus offert gratuito vitam ac salutem per Jesum Christum.*
13 Westminster Confession of Faith 7.3, in Schaff, *Creeds of Christendom*, 3:617; emphasis added.

Davenant men were given latitude for their views and were thus enabled also to sign the confession in the firm conviction that their views were not specifically condemned.

Schaff dealt with this question at some length and concluded that the formulation of the Westminster Confession in 3.6, 7.3, and 8.8

> looks like a compromise between conditional univer- salism taught in the first clause [of 7.3], and particular election taught in the second. This is in substance the theory of the school of Saumur, which was first broached by the Scotch divine, Cameron (d. 1625), and more fully developed by his pupil Amyrault, between AD 1630 and 1650, and which was afterwards condemned in the Hel- vetic Consensus Formula (1675).[14]

In an interesting footnote, Schaff connected all this with the offer, which he espoused:

> The ablest modern defendants of a limited atonement, Drs. Cunningham and Hodge...are as emphatic on the absolute *sufficiency* as Reynolds. Their arguments are chiefly logical; but logic depends on the premises, and is a two-edged sword which may be turned against them as well. For if the atonement be limited in *design,* it must be limited in the *offer;* or if unlimited in [the] offer, the offer made to the non-elect must be *insincere* and *hypocritical,* which is inconsistent with the truth- fulness and goodness of God. Every Calvinist preaches on the assumption that the offer of salvation is truly and

---

14 Ibid., 1:772–73.

sincerely extended to *all* his hearers, and that it is their *own* fault if they are not saved.[15]

Mitchell took the same position.

It is remarkable that, though the Assembly met after the Synod of Dort, and had for its president one whose opinions on these mysterious subjects were almost as pronounced as those of Gomarus himself, it fell back not on the decrees of that Synod, but on the Articles of the Irish Church, which had been drawn up before the Synod of Dort was summoned, or the controversies its decrees occasioned had waxed so fierce. The debates of the Assembly clearly show that its members did not wish to determine several particulars decided by the Synod of Dort, far less to determine them more rigidly than it had done...Did these divines mean to follow an opposite policy in regard to the point on which Calamy, Arrowsmith, Vines, Seaman, and other disciples of Davenant, or according to Baillie of Amyraut, differed from the more exact Calvinists? After repeated perusal of their debates, I cannot take upon myself certainly to affirm that they did, though I admit that this matter is not so clear as the others above referred to.[16]

---

15 Ibid., 1:772, n1. I question that Schaff's last sentence is true of "every Calvinist." It is possible however, that Schaff used "offer of salvation" in the sense of presentation, but that is unlikely, given his views of the well-meant offer.

16 Mitchell and Struthers, *Minutes of the Sessions of the Westminster Assembly*, liv–lv.

Mitchell's conclusion is correct. While some at Westminster defended Amyraldism, it was not incorporated into the Confession, but it was not specifically excluded.[17]

There were probably two reasons for that. First, the Westminster Confession has no negative sections, as do the Canons of Dordt, that condemn specific errors. Second, the exclusion of negative sections was probably due to several factors. The Westminster Confession was not born out of the fire of persecution, as was the Belgic Confession, or out of controversy, as were the Canons of Dordt. This gave the Westminster Confession an objective and somewhat abstract character, far removed from the warmer, more personal tone of the Belgic Confession, which often begins its articles with "We believe." And the Westminster Confession is far removed from the strong pastoral concern of the Canons, which so warmly speak of the personal assurance of the child of God. Within the context of the times, the Parliament, which authorized the Westminster Confession, and the assembly wanted to replace Anglicanism with the doctrines of Westminster as the religion of the state. This intention necessarily involved making the Westminster Confession inclusive rather than exclusive as the confession of the realm.

I can only conclude that the Westminster Confession is weak in failing to exclude certain views promoted by the Davenant men, a failure that enabled men to sign it who remained Amyraldian at heart. It is also weak in failing to define clearly its idea of the well-meant offer, a subject that was an issue among those who defended some form of Amyraldism.[18]

---

17 Herman Hanko, "A Comparison of the Westminster and Reformed Confessions," *Protestant Reformed Theological Journal* 20, no. 1 (November 1986): 3–19.

18 For a further discussion of Davenant's theology, see Mark Shand, "John Davenant: A Jewel of the Reformed Churches or a Tarnished Stone?" in

Yet the positive statements of the Westminster Confession set forth the truth of scripture on all these points and do not, by any stretch of the imagination, incorporate the views of the well-meant offer into its formulation. Any form of Arminianism—also such as represented by Amyraut and Davenant—and the whole notion of the well-meant offer were excluded from the formulation of this great assembly.

I conclude this chapter with a quotation from William Cunningham that clearly shows the difference between Arminianism and Calvinism on the offer of the gospel.

The Arminians, believing in universal grace, in the sense of God's love to all men, that is, *omnibus et singulis,* or His design and purpose to save all men conditionally,—and in universal redemption, or Christ's dying for all men,—consistently follow out these views by asserting a universal *proclamation* to men of God's purpose of mercy,—a universal vocation, or offer and invitation, to men to receive pardon and salvation,—accompanied by a universal sufficient grace,—gracious assistance actually and universally bestowed, sufficient to enable all men, if they choose, to attain to the full possession of spiritual blessings, and ultimately to salvation. Calvinists, while they admit that pardon and salvation are offered indiscriminately to all to whom the gospel is preached, and that all who can be reached should be invited and urged to come to Christ and embrace Him, *deny that this flows from, or indicates, any design or purpose on God's part to save all men;* and without pretending to understand or unfold all the objects or ends of this arrangement,

the *Protestant Reformed Theological Journal* 31, no. 2 (April 1998): 43–69, and 32, no. 1 (November 1998): 20–28.

or to assert that it has no other object or end whatever, regard it as *mainly* designed to effect the result of calling out and saving God's chosen people; and they deny that grace, or gracious divine assistance, sufficient to produce faith and regeneration, is given to all men.[19]

19 William Cunningham, *Historical Theology: A Review of the Principal Doctrinal Discussions in the Christian Church Since the Apostolic Age*, 2nd ed. (Edinburgh: T. and T. Clark, 1864), 2:396–97. The emphasis is Cunningham's except in the phrase that follows "embrace Him."

Chapter 6

THE MARROW
CONTROVERSY

The Marrow controversy was somewhat of a turning point in the history of the church, at least for Presbyterian and Reformed churches. The doctrine of the well-meant offer and some of its corollaries had been taught prior to the Marrow controversy, but the struggle in Scotland, where the Marrow controversy took place, defined the issues and determined subsequent thinking on the all-important subject of the preaching of the gospel.

The Reformation was not as strong in England as it was on the continent of Europe. That was due to the efforts in England to make a Protestant state church out of a Roman Catholic Church, while the Reformation on the continent took place by *separation* from the Roman Catholic Church. Arminianism did not appear in England until 1595, when it was taught by Peter Baro, Margaret Professor of Divinity at Cambridge University. The opposition to his teachings occasioned the formulation and adoption of the Lambeth Articles (1595), which were unofficially added to the Thirty-nine Articles of the Church of England. The

Lambeth Articles specified certain points of doctrine involved in the defense of the truths of sovereign grace over against Arminianism.[1]

However, others taught and defended Baro's views. Amyraldism came into England, and Davenant men taught it and represented it at the Westminster Assembly. Richard Baxter (1615–91) taught the same ideas. He was Grotian in his doctrines of Christ, the atonement, and salvation.[2] He believed it was his calling to fight a certain antinomianism that had appeared in the church, but he became neonomian and taught justification by faith and the works of the new law. The matters of antinomianism and neonomianism occupied an important place in the Marrow controversy.

Baxter was opposed by John Owen especially in his book *The Death of Death in the Death of Christ.*[3] J. I. Packer said that Owen wrote against classical Arminianism, Amyraldism, and the views of Thomas More, the English humanist. He also claimed that Ussher, Davenant, and Baxter, while holding to a modified Amyraldism, had not yet appeared in print with their views at the time Owen wrote his book.[4] Packer correctly insisted that the book is not only about the atonement, but also about the gospel. He answered a question likely to be put to him: "Surely all that Owen is doing is defending limited atonement?" Packer answered as follows:

---

1 For the Lambeth Articles and some explanatory background, see Schaff, *Creeds of Christendom*, 3:658–62.

2 Hugo Grotius taught the governmental theory of the atonement.

3 John Owen, *The Death of Death in the Death of Christ: Being a Treatise of the Redemption and Reconciliation that is in the Blood of Christ; wherein the Whole Controversy about Universal Redemption is Fully Discussed in Four Parts* (Carlisle, PA: George Kline, 1792).

4 J. I. Packer, "Introductory Essay," in John Owen, *The Death of Death in the Death of Christ* (Edinburgh: Banner of Truth Trust, 1967), 23.

Not really. He is doing much more than that. Strictly speaking, the aim of Owen's book is not defensive at all, but constructive. It is a biblical and theological enquiry; its purpose is simply to make clear what Scripture actually teaches about the central subject of the gospel—the achievement of the Saviour. As its title proclaims, it is "a treatise of the redemption and reconciliation that is in the blood of Christ: with the merit thereof, and the satisfaction wrought thereby." The question which Owen, like the Dort divines before him, is really concerned to answer is just this: what is the gospel?[5]

Owen taught that the minister may not preach that Christ died for everyone who hears and that God loves everyone.[6] Man cannot save himself. Christ died for sinners. All who confess sin and believe in Christ will be received. Those who confess sin and believe in Christ are those whom God has chosen from all eternity. All who hear the gospel face repentance and faith as a duty and calling, but to this is always added a particular promise, so that the general command that comes to all men through the preaching is always accompanied by a particular promise made only to those who repent and believe, that is, to the elect.

---

5   Packer, "Introductory Essay," in ibid., 11. Packer's essay is reprinted as "'Saved by His Precious Blood': An Introduction to John Owen's *The Death of Death in the Death of Christ*" in J. I. Packer, *A Quest for Godliness: The Puritan Vision of the Christian Life* (Wheaton, IL: Crossway Books, 1990), 125–148.

6   It would be instructive for modern defenders of the well-meant offer to read what Owen had to say about 2 Peter 3:9, 1 Timothy 2:4, and other texts that are commonly quoted in defense of God's universal purpose to save all men. Owen scoffed at the notion that these texts refer to any but God's elect (John Owen, *The Works of John Owen*, ed. William H. Goold [Edinburgh: Johnstone and Hunter, 1852; repr., Edinburgh: Banner of Truth Trust, 1967], 10:307–16).

Owen said that the preacher's task is to *display* Christ. Packer claimed that Owen held to the offer and an invitation.[7] Owen used those words in the sense of Christ *presented,* Christ *portrayed,* or Christ *set forth* in the gospel—meanings that come directly from the Latin root *offere.* Owen also used the word *invitation,* but he used it in the sense of an invitation of a king, that is, a command from King Jesus to all men who hear the gospel to repent of sin and turn to Christ. Yet Packer insisted that Owen pressed home the idea—so important to Puritan thinking—that God through Christ, with the most tender entreaties and most urgent pleas, urges all sinners to believe.[8] Although Owen wrote before Amyraldism appeared on the scene, he wrote the opposite of what that error taught.

Those issues also occupied the attention of the Marrow men, and they were of particular concern in connection with the dispute over the book *The Marrow of Modern Divinity.*[9]

The first part of the book, which is of particular concern for this book, is written in the form of a conversation between Neophytus, a new convert to the faith; Nomista, who represents antinomianism; and Evangelista, a pastor who speaks the views of the author and expresses what Edward Fisher considered to be the truth on the subject of the relationship of the gospel to antinomianism and neonomianism.

The book did not attract much attention when it was first published, but it came to the attention of the Scottish theologians in the early part of the eighteenth century under interesting

---

7   Packer, *A Quest for Godliness,* 139–40.

8   Ibid., 139, 142.

9   Edward Fisher, *The Marrow of Modern Divinity.* The book was first published in 1645 and republished with an added second part in 1649. A recent edition is Edward Fisher, *The Marrow of Modern Divinity in Two Parts* (Swengel, PA: Reiner Publications, 1978).

circumstances. The Auchterarder Presbytery of the Church of Scotland examined William Craig, a candidate for licensure to the ministry of the gospel. During the examination, he was asked to subscribe to the statement, "I believe that it is not sound and orthodox to teach that we must forsake sin in order to our coming to Christ." Put into simpler language, the statement meant that it was heretical to teach that it is necessary to forsake sin in order to believe in Christ; or to put it another way, orthodoxy says that one can come to Christ without forsaking sin. To this rather strange statement and clumsily worded article of faith, William Craig refused to subscribe, and because he refused to subscribe to it he was denied licensure to the ministry. The matter went to the general assembly of the Church of Scotland for resolution. The statement in question became known as the Auchterarder Creed.

After long discussion, the general assembly made several decisions. First, it ruled that subscription could be required only of statements that the general assembly required. The Auchterarder Presbytery was reprimanded for going beyond anything that the general assembly had required of her ministers. Second, the Auchterarder Creed was condemned as being antinomian, because it taught that repentance was not necessary to come to Christ. Third, the assembly also warned against the evils of denying the need for holiness (antinomianism) and the teaching that good works are the basis for salvation (neonomianism).

While the assembly condemned the Auchterarder Creed, the Auchterarder Presbytery was not disciplined, because the members of the presbytery gave the creed a good interpretation, namely, that one must come to Christ with his sins to obtain pardon for them, or else there was no point in coming to Christ. While the general assembly accepted that interpretation, it nevertheless insisted that the wording of the creed was capable of an antinomian meaning and ought to be condemned.

During the discussions of this matter, Thomas Boston, a delegate famous for his book *Human Nature in Its Fourfold State*, leaned over and whispered to John Drummond that he knew of a book that admirably answered all the points under discussion. He referred to *The Marrow of Modern Divinity*, which he had picked up at a friend's house and read with great enjoyment. Shortly after the general assembly concluded its meetings, those who were impressed with the content of that book republished it.

Because of its popularity and doubtful teachings, the book soon came under official scrutiny, and the general assembly of the Church of Scotland officially treated the content of the book in 1720. The assembly condemned the book for the following reasons: First, it held that assurance is of the nature of faith, contrary to the Westminster Confession of Faith. Second, it taught a universal atonement and pardon in the cross.[10] Third, it taught that holiness is not necessary to salvation. Fourth, it taught that the fear of punishment and the hope of reward are not allowed to be motives of obedience. Fifth, it held that the believer is not under the law as a rule of life.

While it is clear that the book was condemned particularly for its antinomian teaching, the major point of concern for this book is the second point concerning the relationship between the atonement of Christ and the well-meant offer of the gospel. However, behind that issue of the well-meant offer of the gospel were many other issues that are somewhat helpful to understand the controversy.

The Presbyterian Church of Scotland, the church of John

---

10 While this point was not specifically discussed in the book, the general assembly considered it a necessary part of the teaching of *The Marrow of Modern Divinity* that the universal offer of the gospel was a warrant to each man to receive Christ. At that critical point the offer of salvation entered the discussion.

Knox and Andrew Melville, had followed the pattern of decline into dead orthodoxy and worldliness of the state church in the Netherlands. Countless people were members of the church only because they were citizens of a country where a state church held sway. They were baptized, christened, married, and buried by the church, but little else. They were worldly and carnal. False doctrine was tolerated and in some instances defended without the disapproval of presbyteries and general assemblies. The preaching was more academic than spiritual food for hungry souls. Those weaknesses the Marrow men protested.

At the same time the Marrow men charged the state church with becoming careless and profane in its emphasis on justification alone without the works of the law and on the basis of eternal election. In a way that was the pot calling the kettle black, for the charge of antinomianism that the general assembly leveled against the Marrow men was a just charge—as was clear from the Auchterarder Creed.

The charge of the Marrow men was not necessarily true, for it is historically true that those who criticize justification by faith alone as leading to spiritual carelessness do so out of their unwillingness to accept the doctrine itself. Paul faced that charge already in his day (Rom. 6:1).

Further, the Marrow men charged that the state church could preach only to the elect because of its denial of the well-meant offer. The argument was that because the church said the promise of the gospel is only for the elect, the preaching of the gospel can be only for the elect. The argument was patently false and an excuse to change the gospel into a sincere expression of God's love for the whole human race. That was similar to the present-day charge that those who deny the well-meant offer of the gospel are hyper-Calvinists.

Many in the church were dissatisfied with the general

assembly's condemnation of *The Marrow of Modern Divinity.* Twelve men, later called the Marrow men, protested that decision. The twelve included the well-known theologians Thomas Boston, James Hog, Ralph Erskine, and Ebenezer Erskine. A commission was appointed to examine the protest of the Marrow men.

During the investigation it became evident that the Marrow men, among other things, had claimed that in condemning the universal offer of salvation, the general assembly had condemned the divine command to preach salvation through the Lord Jesus Christ to all men. It also became evident that the Marrow men, while denying that they taught universal atonement, nevertheless taught that the atoning work of Christ was universal in some sense. They distinguished between a gift of Christ in possession and a gift of Christ that warranted men to receive him. The former they limited to the elect; the latter was for all men. They also maintained that the statement "Christ died for all" is clearly heretical, but it is sound and orthodox to teach that Christ is dead for all.

Yet the sources of antinomianism versus neonomianism, while important as background, gradually ceased to be discussed.

When the commission reported to the general assembly in 1722, the original decision of 1720 was maintained, and the Marrow men were once again condemned for their views. By that decision, the general assembly of the Church of Scotland officially condemned the idea of the well-meant offer of the gospel. Therefore, all the Scottish Presbyterian churches that trace their origin to the Church of Scotland are bound by that decision. In the interests of maintaining the well-meant offer, some have denied this, but the evidence supports the contention. The decision of 1720, reaffirmed in 1722, has never been retracted.[11]

---

11 See Evangelical Presbyterian Church of Australia, *Universalism and the Reformed Churches*, 7–8.

Various interpretations have been given to the Marrow controversy, some of which are efforts to justify the theology of the Marrow men. Usually these interpretations attempt to put the blame for heresy on the Presbyterian church, and they present the Marrow position as a necessary corrective of evils.

While I do not deny that many evils were present in the church, it must be said in defense of the general assembly that it did not teach legalism as is claimed, but specifically and concretely warned against it. Who can tell whether there were those in the church who were teaching such views? It is possible that some were guilty, but the fact is that the general assembly, which had condemned the offer, refused to uphold legalism and warned against it. The general assembly was not guilty of teaching conditional salvation, as some claim. That is a misinterpretation of the assembly's position. The assembly insisted that the promises of the gospel were for the elect alone and that these promises were to be publicly and universally proclaimed along with the command to repent and believe. Thus the assembly maintained a general proclamation of a particular promise in the same sense as Dordt had maintained it.[12]

That doctrine had always been considered biblical and Reformed. It is true that the promise of the gospel is for the elect alone. It is also true that a holy and sanctified life is the fruit of election as God works his sanctifying power in the hearts of his people through the Spirit of Christ. We may even say that only in the way of a sanctified walk can the elect child of God live in the assurance of his election in Christ. Certainly no Christian would ever dare to say that a person can walk in sin, refuse to confess it, and experience the electing grace of God in Christ. Yet saying this by no means implies conditional salvation.

---

12 Canons of Dordt 2.5, in *Confessions and Church Order,* 163.

By agreeing with the general assembly's decision to condemn the Marrow men, I am not saying that the Church of Scotland was orthodox in all things. In the case of the Marrow men, the church was right, but many unsound doctrines and practices remained.

Contrary to the above allegations, the Marrow men taught conditional salvation. If salvation merited in Christ's work on the cross is publicly proclaimed as being for all men, the question naturally arises, how is it to be explained that not all men actually receive salvation? The only answer that can possibly be given—the answer given by the Marrow men—is that salvation comes to an individual on the *condition* of faith. Only those who fulfill the condition of believing become the heirs of salvation.

In defense of a well-meant offer of the gospel, the Marrow men taught that Christ's atonement, upon which the offer rested, was universal in some sense. They said that the offer expressed God's universal love for all men and his desire to save all men. The salvation that men received, therefore, was salvation dependent upon man's act of faith.

John Macleod and C. G. M'Crie took a slightly different position.[13] They maintained that a certain hyper-Calvinism had come into the Church of Scotland from the Netherlands, which had the chief characteristic that the call of the gospel and its promises are for the elect only. According to such hyper-Calvinism, the gospel cannot come to a man who cannot receive it, because responsibility is limited to and by a man's

---

13 John Macleod, *Scottish Theology in Relation to Church History since the Reformation* (Free Church of Scotland, 1943; repr., Edinburgh: Banner of Truth Trust, 1974), 133–38, 143–68, 175–80. See also J. I. Packer, "Arminianisms," in *The Manifold Grace of God*, and C. G. M'Crie, introduction, in Edward Fisher, *The Marrow of Modern Divinity in Two Parts*, C. G. M'Crie, ed. (Glasgow: David Bryce & Son, 1902), xxvii–xxviii.

ability. According to Macleod and M'Crie, the hyper-Calvinistic position that the gospel can only be preached to the elect is essentially Arminian, except the Arminians broadened the concept of ability far more than the hyper-Calvinists. In opposition to that, the Marrow men taught a universal love of God and a universal offer of the gospel. Christ therefore belonged to all men—not in possession but in the free and well-meant offer.[14]

While Macleod and M'Crie presented the position of the Marrow men in an essentially correct way, they confused the history and occasion of the controversy. Without any proof they branded as hyper-Calvinism the idea that the *promise* of the gospel is and can be limited only to the elect. They confused the *preaching* of the *promise* of God with the *promise* itself and claimed that to make the promise only for the elect means that the preaching of the promise is also for the elect only.

To claim that the *preaching* of the promise is for the elect only is not and never was orthodox Calvinism. That the *promise* of God is for the elect only is the traditional view of the church and her theologians from the time of Calvin. The Reformed have also insisted that the particular promise of God must be promiscuously preached so that all who hear may know that promise. In the preaching God promises salvation only to those who believe, for God will not promise salvation to unbelievers. God does not promise salvation to those he does not intend to save. But the promiscuous *preaching* of that particular promise is accompanied by the command to all men to repent and believe in Christ, in whom alone is found salvation. If the promiscuous preaching of a particular promise is hyper-Calvinism, then the

---

14 This is also the essential position of Ernest F. Kevan, *The Grace of Law: A Study in Puritan Theology* (London: Carey Kingsgate Press; repr., Grand Rapids, MI: Baker Book House, 1965), 89, n84.

Synod of Dordt was composed of hyper-Calvinists, as was Calvin himself.

The orthodox in the Church of Scotland maintained that the promise of salvation in Christ is particular and therefore is not made to those who reject it. But the Marrow men were wrong in interpreting that position to mean that because the promise of the gospel is particular, the gospel cannot be preached to all men. The gospel includes the command to all men to repent and to believe in Christ.

The Church of Scotland did not teach that man's responsibility is limited to and by his ability. The Reformed have always maintained that all men are responsible before God for their sins, and their responsibility has nothing to do with their ability. Exactly because of man's responsibility, the command of the gospel confronts all men with their obligation to forsake sin and to repent at the foot of the cross.

The Evangelical Presbyterian Church of Australia presented a third interpretation, which is the correct one, by maintaining that the Marrow controversy was a direct result of Davenant's view of the atonement and the offer, which continued to be taught in the churches in Great Britain because the Westminster Assembly had not specifically condemned it. This weakness of the Westminster Confession was corrected by the Church of Scotland in its condemnation of the Marrow men in 1720 and 1722. According to the Evangelical Presbyterian Church, the Marrow men taught a modified Calvinism that has been the scourge of the church to the present.[15]

The point in the Marrow controversy that particularly concerns this book is the nature of the preaching of the gospel. The

15 Evangelical Presbyterian Church of Australia, *Universalism and the Reformed Churches*, 5–10.

controversy arose in connection with a view of preaching that was fairly common in the British Isles, especially among some of the Puritans. In the latter half of the sixteenth century, the Puritans considered the partial reformation of the church to be inadequate and condemned worldliness in the church. In their opposition to those weaknesses, they tended to stress strongly the subjective elements in the Christian life, and the stress on these subjective elements led to a view of preaching found in many of their pulpits.

The Puritans stressed the importance of preaching the law as a means God uses to prepare men for true conversion. All Puritans did not completely agree with that, and there was some development among them on the matter. Especially some of the later Puritans taught that the preaching of the law is accompanied by certain gracious influences of God in the hearts of the unregenerate, which God uses to bring men to know their sins and to recognize themselves as sinners. The preaching of the law is accompanied by a preparatory grace that is to be sharply distinguished from saving grace. Preparatory grace is given to everyone who hears the preaching, but it does not save anyone. Preparatory grace is necessary to salvation, but it does not guarantee salvation. It effects in the hearer a conviction of sin under which a person may labor for a long time. He is burdened with his sin and guilt, troubled by an incessantly plaguing conscience that moves him to seek relief from the grief brought about by his sins.[16]

The people who labored under the conviction of sin were sometimes called "seekers" to emphasize that they earnestly sought peace of heart and relief from their anguished grief over sin. In that state they were able to pray, even for regeneration and conversion, and to attend church to hear the gospel as it

---

16 Helm, *Calvin and the Calvinists*, 61–70.

presented Christ who came to save sinners. Although seeking could continue for years, it might not result in conversion, and the seeker would be lost.[17]

Norman Pettit wrote lucidly of the inherent Arminianism of Puritan preparationism. He described preparationists as maintaining that "contrition and humiliation were not in themselves saving graces but preliminary steps, and that while God takes away all resistance, this cannot be done without man's consent."[18] Then Pettit wrote concerning the Puritan teaching of man's relationship to God's covenant:

> If God's will was always omnipotent, still He looked to the inner man for the "new heart" required in the new covenant. If God alone sought out those to be taken, man had always to "choose" God by entering the covenant voluntarily.[19]

Pettit quoted Richard Sibbes: "If we regard ourselves, we are his by voluntary acceptance of the covenant of grace."[20]

Describing New England Puritanism, Pettit said,

> No point in New England theology was more significant for religious introspection than how much a man could do under the Law to predispose himself for saving grace, or how much through preparation he could dispose God to save him...Yet all were told, at the same

---

17 For an interesting and instructive description of the effect of Puritan preaching, see Kenneth MacRae, *Diary of Kenneth MacRae: A Record of Fifty Years in the Christian Ministry*, ed. Iain H. Murray (Edinburgh: Banner of Truth Trust, 1980).

18 Norman Pettit, *The Heart Prepared: Grace and Conversion in Puritan Spiritual Life*, 2nd ed. (Middletown, CT: Wesleyan University Press, 1989), 18.

19 Ibid., 13.

20 Ibid., 14.

time, that no matter how much they prepared, no matter how thoroughly they searched beneath the surface of human appearances, God's mercy could be denied in the end. The prepared heart, while a necessary prerequisite to the conversion experience, was no guarantee of salvation.[21]

The Synod of Dordt had already rejected the error of those who teach

> that the unregenerate man is not really nor utterly dead in sin, nor destitute of all powers unto spiritual good, but that he can yet hunger and thirst after righteousness and life, and offer the sacrifice of a contrite and broken spirit, which is pleasing to God.
>
> Rejection: For these are contrary to the express testimony of Scripture, Ye were dead through trespasses and sins (Eph. 2:1, 5); and: Every imagination of the thoughts of his heart was only evil continually (Gen. 6:5; 8:21).
>
> Moreover, to hunger and thirst after deliverance from misery and after life, and to offer unto God the sacrifice of a broken spirit, is peculiar to the regenerate and those that are called blessed (Ps. 51:10, 19; Matt. 5:6).[22]

While the Dordt theologians addressed the Arminian error, which was slightly different from the Puritan error of preparationism, the clear similarity is striking. The Arminians and the Puritans praised the actions that the Canons say cannot be done by the unregenerated, and both explained these actions as a grace of God given to everyone who hears the gospel. Basically, therefore, the Puritan view was condemned by the Synod of Dordt.

---

21 Ibid., 18–19.
22 Canons 3–4, error and rejection 4, in *Confessions and Church Order*, 171.

Puritan preaching was addressed to the "seeking" spiritual state of many Puritans. The preaching was often an offer to encourage those who were under the conviction of sin to embrace the gospel. The preaching portrayed God's mercy with the intention of disarming the most alienated mind of his suspicions and of relieving the most troubled spirit of his fears. It was intended to assure the hearers that no sinner had sunk beyond the reach of mercy, and that no sins were so great that they were beyond forgiveness. Thus earnest entreaties and tender remonstrances were necessary to bring the sinner to Christ.[23]

That idea led to various degrees of seeking. Some had a felt need; they hungered and thirsted and were weary and heavy laden. Others had not even progressed that far. The first were under more serious pressures to close with Christ than the others.

There were also various degrees in the conviction of sin. The question often arose whether a sinner was truly and sufficiently under the conviction of sin, or whether his conviction was only apparent and not a genuine matter of the heart.

There were also distinctions in the assurance of faith. A sinner might not presume to be elect or conclude that he was not elect. The assurance that he was elect went through various stages until he stood in the full assurance of his salvation in Christ.

In addition, the Marrow controversy was carried on with a wrong idea of the covenant. God's covenant is certainly and unconditionally established with his elect people in the line of generations, for God's promise is to believers and their seed (Gen. 17:7; Acts 2:39). But it was common doctrine in Presbyterian circles that the children of believers were to be considered

---

23 Thomas J. Crawford, *The Doctrine of the Holy Scripture respecting the Atonement,* 4th ed. (Grand Rapids, MI: Baker Book House, 1954), 141–47.

as unconverted until they could believe in Christ as adults. If the biblical doctrine of the covenant that God saves the elect children of believers would have been maintained, preparationism would never have arisen.

What did all that have to do with the idea of the well-meant offer of the gospel?

The word *offer* had been used frequently prior to the Marrow controversy. It was used by the Westminster divines in the Westminster Confession, and it was used by John Owen and other Puritan divines. Usually it meant the setting forth of Christ as the one who had come as the savior from sin. But as the need grew for pressing home the sufficiency of the cross of Christ upon the man convicted of sin, the meaning shifted to that proposed by the Marrow men, who taught that no man need doubt the "warrant," or legal right, to receive the Savior's blessings. Everyone who hears the preaching has a warrant to receive and embrace the gospel. No living man has a warrant to refuse. God expresses in the gospel his desire to save everyone, and this is the only way the gospel can be pressed home upon one convicted of sin. The sinner has a legal right to the blessings of Christ's suffering because in some way Christ died for him, and God loves him and desires his salvation.

In the light of the Puritan error, this view is somewhat understandable. Under the preaching of the law, the unregenerate sinner who has been convicted of sin and cries out for relief from the oppression of sin and guilt has to be assured that Christ desires his salvation and that the gospel, which presents Christ crucified, is indeed for him. That precise emphasis led to the teaching of a certain universality of the atonement.

The passages in *The Marrow of Modern Divinity* that had come under the scrutiny of the general assembly of the Church of Scotland read as follows:

God the Father, as he is in his Son Jesus Christ, moved with nothing but his free love to mankind lost, hath made a deed of gift and grant unto them all, that whosoever of them all shall believe in this his Son, shall not perish, but have eternal life…Go and tell every man without exception that here are good news for him; Christ is dead for him, and if he will take him, and accept his righteousness he shall have him.[24]

C. G. M'Crie stated that the Marrow men maintained that "gospel giving is not giving into possession, but giving by way of offer."[25] M'Crie also said that in 1742 those men expressed themselves thus: "There is a revelation of the Divine will in the Word, affording a warrant to offer Christ unto all mankind without exception, and a warrant to all freely to receive Him, however great sinners they are or have been."[26]

Alexander A. Hodge, writing in the latter half of the nineteenth century, defined the issues in the Marrow controversy very clearly. He said that the Marrow men spoke of a "double reference" of the atonement. Their desire was to establish the "*Warrant of Faith.*"[27] According to the Marrow men,

the atonement had a designed general reference to all sinners of mankind as such…Christ did not die for all men—that is, to save all—yet…he is dead for all, that is,

24 Edward Fisher, *The Marrow of Modern Divinity in Two Parts* (Swengel, PA: Reiner Publications, 1976), 126–27.

25 C. G. M'Crie, *The Confessions of the Church of Scotland: Their Evolution in History, Seventh Series of the Chalmers Lectures* (Edinburgh: Macniven & Wallace, 1907), 125.

26 Ibid.

27 Archibald Alexander Hodge, *The Atonement* (Philadelphia, PA: Presbyterian Board of Publication, 1867), 380.

available for all if they will receive him...God, out of his general philanthropy, or love for human sinners as such, had made a Deed of Gift of Christ and the benefits of his redemption to all indifferently, to be claimed upon the condition of faith. This general love of God is styled his "giving love," and is distinguished from his "electing love," of which only the elect...are objects. This Deed of Gift or Grant of Christ to all sinners as such, they [the Marrow men] held, is not to be merely resolved into the general offer of the gospel, but is to be regarded as the foundation upon which that general offer rests. It is a real grant; universal; an expression of love; conditioned on faith...and it is the "warrant"upon which the faith of every believer rests, and by which faith is justified. [28]

John Macleod said that Guthrie of Fenwick taught the following concerning the Marrow doctrine:

That though none cordially close with God in Christ Jesus, and acquiesce in that ransom found out by God, except only such as are elected, and whose heart the Lord doth sovereignly determine to that blessed choice, yet the Lord has left it as a duty upon people who hear His Gospel to close with His offer of salvation, as if it were in their power to do it.[29]

From all this, the central issues in the Marrow controversy are clear.

First, preaching involves a conception of conversion and faith different from historic Reformed theology. For the Marrow men, conversion in the line of the covenant is essentially no

---

28 Ibid., 381–82.
29 Guthrie, quoted in John Macleod, *Scottish Theology*, 181.

different from conversion effected among the unchurched. Conversion does not occur in infancy but later in life and is preceded by a conviction of sin that is not the work of saving grace. The conviction of sin results from the preaching and an accompanying preparatory grace, which brings a man into a state in which he hungers and thirsts for righteousness and seeks escape from the burden of sin and guilt that afflicts his tortured conscience. This view of preparatory grace introduced into the thinking of the church a certain common grace that was responsible for assigning acts to the unregenerate that scripture assigns only to the regenerate child of God.

Second, the Marrow men claimed that the offer of the gospel was necessary so that the troubled sinner could have no reason for refusing to come to Christ. For them the offer was not only the proclamation that sets forth Christ as the God-ordained way of salvation, but also a warrant to believe in Christ. The Marrow men wanted to press home the demands of faith by giving everyone the *right* to believe in Christ. Everyone has not only the obligation to believe, but also the right to believe. He has the right to believe because salvation is available for him, and Christ is available for him because Christ is dead for all men. In that way they urged upon sinners the blessedness of finding salvation from sin in Christ. Thus the offer expresses God's earnest desire to save all men. It reveals God's intention to make all men partakers of Christ. It speaks of God's love that extends to all men.

Third, by their distinction between the statements "Christ died for all" and "Christ is dead for all," the Marrow men made the atonement universal in a certain sense. They denied that Christ died for all men, but they maintained that Christ is dead for all men. The atonement was sufficient for all men, and God intended atonement for all, because it is a manifestation of his universal love for all men. Thus the atonement established the warrant for all men to believe. In this way the atonement was made available for all.

Fourth, the Marrow men's views of predestination were essentially Amyraldian: the counsel of God with respect to predestination contains a determinative decree and a hypothetical decree. The determinative decree belongs to God's secret will, and the hypothetical decree belongs to God's revealed will. Especially the hypothetical decree is proclaimed through the preaching. The revealed will of God expresses God's will as desiring the salvation of all who hear the gospel.

Finally, all of those conceptions introduced a conditional salvation into the work of God. The Marrow men claimed that by making salvation conditioned upon faith, they made the work of salvation particular, because only the elect come to faith. Actually they made the whole work of salvation dependent upon man's work of faith. Some only are saved, although God desires the salvation of all men, earnestly urges them all to come to Christ, and provides an atonement that is sufficient, intended, and available for all men. Why, then, do not all come? The Marrow answer was that all men do not come to Christ because all of them do not exercise saving faith. But if God wants them to be saved, and they do not believe, the choice of believing or not believing is their choice.

The Marrow men did teach that saving faith is worked by God in the hearts of the elect of God. By saying that, they hoped to escape the charge of Arminianism. But their statement did not work for them for two reasons.

First, how is it to be explained that God desires to save all men and expresses his desire in the preaching of the gospel, but God actually gives faith and salvation only to a select few? To resolve that dilemma, the Marrow men, like the Amyraldians, resorted to a distinction in the will of God. In one will God wills to save all men; in the other will God desires to save only some. That distinction sets God in opposition to himself.

Second, by making faith the condition of salvation, the Marrow men set faith outside the work of salvation. If it is true that God desires to save all men but only those who believe are saved, it is also true that the blessings of salvation are dependent upon faith. Then faith cannot be a blessing of salvation, but is a condition to salvation. One cannot have it both ways. Faith is either part of salvation or a condition to salvation, but both it cannot be. In separating faith from the benefits of salvation, as the Marrow men necessarily had to do, they made faith the work of man. No pious talk of faith as the work of God could alter that fundamental claim.

The Evangelical Presbyterian Church of Australia is correct when it finds the following "ambiguities" in Marrow thought:

1. "Christ has taken upon Him the sins of all men," and "being a deed of gift and grant unto all mankind," is not a universal purchase of the death of Christ, therefore it logically follows that,

2. [T]he said deed of gift and grant of Christ to all mankind is effective only to the elect, i.e., an infallible redemption gifted to all secures only a portion of its objects.

3. A deed of gift and grant to all is only an offer. In other words, Christ is gifted to all, without that He died for them.

4. Since the gift of Christ to all is not a benefit purchased by the atonement, the substance of the free offer of the gospel does not consist of Christ as redeemer, but only as a friend.[30]

---

30 Evangelical Presbyterian Church, *Universalism and the Reformed Faith*, 9–10.

The Marrow men were rightly condemned by several general assemblies of the Scottish churches. The Marrow party had attempted to introduce into the church ideas that were foreign to the historic faith of Calvinism and had attempted to bring the church into an Amyraldian theological position. That the Marrow men could have had such influence on subsequent Presbyterian thought is hard to understand, especially since their views were condemned by their own church. Those Presbyterians who have roots in the Scottish churches ought to take note that insofar as they teach the offer as maintained by the Marrow men, they run contrary to their church's adopted theological position.

Chapter 7

⟽⟼

LATER PRESBYTERIAN THOUGHT

A completely worked out system of the theology of the well-meant offer of the gospel did not appear within Presbyterian churches for many years. When it did finally appear and was on the official agenda of the church, it was found only in some Presbyterian bodies. Many Presbyterian thinkers discussed the offer and even adopted the language of the offer, but in important instances they opposed the theology of the offer or were ambiguous in what precisely they meant by it. Since I cannot discuss every Presbyterian thinker, I choose to discuss only some representative thinkers of more recent times whose influence has been significant in modern Presbyterian thought.

The well-meant offer at times arose in official discussions of Presbyterian churches. An example of such a case was noted in 1984 by Maurice Roberts in an article on John Kennedy (1819–84).[1] The article treats, among many other things, the role that

---

1   Maurice Roberts, "Dr. John Kennedy—A Memorial Sketch," *Banner of Truth* 251–52 (August–September 1984): 1–31. Kennedy was the minister

Kennedy, of the Free Church of Scotland, played in the negotiations that began in the 1860s between the Free Church of Scotland and the United Presbyterians regarding their possible union. Especially two differences were discussed in connection with those negotiations: the relationship of the civil magistrate to the church of Christ and the extent of Christ's atonement. In connection with the atonement, the subject of the offer was discussed.

The thinking of many United Presbyterians at that time about the extent of the atonement can be fairly estimated from the following quotations from some of their spokesmen: "It is impossible for any man to preach the gospel who preaches a limited atonement." "The work of Christ has provided salvation for all men indiscriminately." "The universal offer of the Gospel has its basis in the general reference of the work of Christ." "Christ's death made all men salvable." "The grace of God is manifested to sinners indiscriminately in the provision and offer of the gospel."[2]

Roberts summed up the attitude of the United Presbyterian synod in two propositions: "The love of God, as expressed in the gift and death of the Son, was not love to the elect exclusively." "Christ died for all men, according to a divine intention, as, in some sense, their substitute, and with a view to procuring salvability, if not salvation, for them."[3]

Kennedy objected to those views, and with him stood such outstanding men as Robert Smith, Robert Candlish, Robert Haldane, and William Cunningham. They appealed to an 1804

---

of the Free Church of Scotland in Dingwall in the Scottish Highlands from 1843 until his death in 1884.

2   Roberts, "Dr. John Kennedy—A Memorial Sketch," 23. The spokesmen were not identified.

3   Ibid.

decision of the general associate synod of the United Secession Church, which had stated the following:

> Christ died for the elect, and for them only. The death of Christ, possessing infinite merit, is, indeed, in itself sufficient for the redemption of all mankind. But in respect of the Father's assignation, and his own intention, He died only for the elect...All for whom Christ died shall be infallibly saved...We therefore condemn, and testify against the following error...that Christ died in some sense for all men.[4]

It is interesting to observe that Kennedy accused the United Presbyterian Church of Amyraldism, and he firmly believed that Amyraldism was present in the church because of the teachings of the Marrow men, particularly with respect to faith. As quoted in the Roberts article, Kennedy had written the following:

> I believe that, in the Marrow definition of faith, there was the germ of all errors which have been developed in Amyraldism, which...is the fashion of the United Presbyterian theology.
>
> That definition implied that the sinner, before believing, had a certain right of property in the Gospel salvation, because of "a deed of gift and grant" from God. This mistaken idea is the most marked thing of all they retain of inherited theology. It is the search for a basis, for this pre-believing right, that has carried them to the universal reference of the atonement, and to their dreamings of universal grace.[5]

---

4   Roberts, "Dr. John Kennedy—A Memorial Sketch," 24.
5   Ibid., 22. Quoted from John Kennedy, *Unionism and the Union* (Edinburgh: J. Maclaren, 1870).

In support of his position, Kennedy quoted from Robert Candlish:

> In Scottish theology, for example, any departure from the strict view of the extent of the atonement is to be seriously dreaded, because it almost uniformly indicates a lurking tendency to call in question the sovereignty of divine grace altogether. Here it is invariably found to open a door for the influx of the entire tide of the Pelagian theory of human ability, in the train of that Arminian notion of the divine decrees which is apt to be its precursor.[6]

From this it is clear that Presbyterians struggled repeatedly with those central issues. It is also clear that the doctrines of the extent of the atonement and the well-meant offer of the gospel were inseparably linked. Where the well-meant offer was taught, universality of the atonement inevitably went along with it. As Candlish pointed out, that was always interwoven with the Pelagian and Arminian heresies. It is sad that Presbyterianism of modern times has failed to see this.

Undoubtedly one of the greatest theologians in modern Presbyterianism was Charles Hodge, whose *Systematic Theology* has had as much influence on present-day Presbyterian thought as any other work.[7] In his writing on the effectual calling, Charles Hodge was not clear on what precisely he meant by the offer. He rejected the theology of the offer, especially the idea that it is God's intention, desire, or purpose to save all who hear the gospel. In everything he said on the subject of the calling,

---

6   Ibid., 25. Quoted from Kennedy, *Unionism and the Union*.
7   Charles Hodge, *Systematic Theology*, 3 vols. (New York: Charles Scribner and Company, 1871–73).

he never spoke of the concept of a well-meant offer of the gospel. Furthermore, he seemed to limit the idea of the offer to the command of the gospel, especially when he stated that "the general call of the gospel is not inconsistent with the doctrine of predestination."[8]

Hodge's clearest opposition to an offer that expresses a universal desire on God's part to save all men is in his repudiation of Lutheranism. He correctly defined the Lutheran position as including a call of the gospel as an expression of God's desire and intent to save all who hear, which are the purpose and goal God has in view.[9] This Lutheran idea lies at the heart of the offer and has been accepted in recent times by almost all who hold to an offer.

Hodge would have none of that. He gave a lengthy refutation of that view and made the following points: First, God's intentions must always come to pass. If this were not so, it would be inconsistent with the divine being. Second, God's purpose cannot fail or be resisted. Hence, if it were God's intention or purpose to save all men, all would be saved. Third, the Lutheran view denies that the ultimate reason for refusing the gospel is God's eternal and unchangeable purpose. Therefore, this view ultimately denies reprobation. Fourth, the Lutheran position has no support in scripture. Here Hodge referred to scriptural passages often quoted in support of the offer, but which he showed do not teach the offer at all.[10]

From this one would conclude that Charles Hodge was an enemy of the well-meant offer and rejected it as heresy. But there are other elements in his treatment of effectual calling that

---

8   Hodge, *Systematic Theology*, 2:643.
9   Ibid., 2:649–52, 656–657.
10 Ibid., 2:649–653.

make one wonder. Sometimes Hodge seemed to want some kind of offer after all; at other times he was unclear and seemed to have no definite conclusions. When he discussed the external call of the gospel, he interpreted the call to include a command, exhortation, or invitation to accept the offered mercy and to exhibit the reasons men ought to come to Christ. While his writing could be interpreted so that it stands in harmony with other statements that condemn the theology of the offer, Hodge dashed such hopes when he interpreted 1 Timothy 2:3–4 to mean that God intends, or purposes, that all men should be saved because he delights in the happiness of his creatures.[11]

Hodge was also ambivalent in discussion of the idea of common, or general, grace. He defined "common grace" as "that influence of the Spirit, which in a greater or less measure, is granted to all who hear the truth." Then he mentioned "sufficient grace," by which he meant "such kind and degree of the Spirit's influence, as is sufficient to lead men to repentance, faith, and a holy life." He also spoke of "preventing grace," by which he meant "that operation of the Spirit on the mind which precedes and excites its efforts to return to God."[12] By these graces the Spirit works in the hearts of all who hear the gospel to convict them of sin, to resist evil in their hearts, to strive and warn, and to convict them of the truth.[13]

While Hodge did not directly connect those ideas of general grace with the well-meant offer of the gospel, historically that has been the case. This was true of the Marrow controversy and of subsequent thought in Presbyterian and Reformed continental theology. The connection is that by general grace given to

---

11 Ibid., 2:651–52.
12 Ibid., 2:654.
13 Ibid., 2:654–75.

all who hear the gospel God shows his willingness and desire to save all men, and by general grace he gives everyone who hears the gospel the spiritual strength to accept or reject Christ offered in the gospel. Those two ideas belong so closely together that it is impossible to separate them.

In the light of those conflicting opinions, it is difficult to judge with certainty Hodge's thinking. Perhaps the best I can say is that while he emphatically repudiated the offer, he seemed to want to retain some idea of it. But to harmonize those two aspects of his thought is impossible.

What was true of Charles Hodge was also true of his son, Archibald Alexander Hodge (1823–86). We need not say much about his work because he followed his father for the most part, even on the matter of common grace. However, in his book *The Atonement*, A. A. Hodge made the following astounding and unwarranted statement:[14]

> It [the external call] is addressed to the non-elect equally with the elect, because it is equally their duty and interest to accept the gospel, because the provisions of salvation are equally suited to their case, and abundantly sufficient for all, *and because God intends that its benefits shall actually accrue to every one who accepts it.*[15]

With some effort even this quotation could be interpreted as being biblical.

The idea of the well-meant offer came to fuller expression in the writings of John Murray (1896–1975). Murray wrote, "The universality of the demand for repentance implies the universal overture of grace…This is the full and unrestricted offer of the

---

14 Hodge, *The Atonement*, 371–72.
15 Hodge, *Outlines of Theology*, 446; emphasis added.

gospel to all men."[16] Did Murray mean that the universal overture of grace and the full and unrestricted offer of the gospel was
the command to all men to repent of sin and believe in Christ?

When Murray discussed the relationship between the
offer and the atonement, his ideas were somewhat clearer. He
insisted that a universal offer must imply a certain universality
in redemption. He defined the universal aspect of redemption as
the many benefits Jesus merited on the cross for the non-elect,
including the blessing of the gospel.[17]

There are many questions that one could ask at this point. Is
it not obvious that Murray meant more by an unrestricted offer
than merely the command to repent and believe in Christ? After
all, there is no need for the redemptive work of Christ to be a
basis for the demand of the gospel to repent and believe.

Another question is, how is it possible for the redeeming
and atoning sacrifice of Christ on the cross to merit blessings
for the non-elect if these blessings are non-saving? It seems that
according to Murray the sacrifice of Christ is actually non-redeeming and non-saving for some for whom Christ actually
died. Does it not follow that Christ died only to make salvation
possible for all men? Or did Christ perform two works on the
cross—one redeeming and saving and the other non-redeeming
and non-saving? The Arminians have answered this question
by asserting that the death of Christ on the cross was only a
sacrifice that makes salvation *available* to all men. This is the
usual conclusion when the well-meant offer is taught and connected with the atonement. Just as importantly, where in all of
scripture is there one statement that so much as suggests that

16 John Murray, "The Atonement and the Free Offer of the Gospel," in John
Murray, *The Collected Writings of John Murray*, vol. 1, *Claims of Truth*
(Edinburgh: Banner of Truth Trust, 1976), 60.
17 Ibid., 62–63.

Christ died to merit blessings for the non-elect, who in fact are not actually saved?

As Murray developed the idea of blessings for the non-elect, he clarified what he meant. The power of a cross that does not actually save but merits blessings for the non-elect implies God's love for the non-elect, which is the source of many blessings and is most highly expressed in "the entreaties, overtures, and demands of the gospel proclamation."[18] While God's love offered in the gospel is not saving, it is real love that expresses God's willingness to save all who hear the gospel.[19]

Regarding the faith that the gospel demands, Murray distinguished between faith people have that God loves *them* and faith that is commitment to Christ. With the faith that is commitment to Christ, the gospel cannot declare indiscriminately that Christ died for every man. Nevertheless, there is an indiscriminate warrant of faith that every sinner possesses. This warrant is not a personal assurance of salvation, but is a warrant in the all-sufficiency of the Savior and the suitability of his atoning sacrifice.

It ought to be evident from the above that Murray was unclear on that point. He emphatically insisted on an offer but shied away from many of the implications of the offer. He tended somewhat toward the Marrow position when he spoke of the warrant of faith, but he did not seem to go as far as the Marrow men. He wanted a universal overture of grace and an unrestricted offer to all men, but he never gave a clear and precise definition of those terms. He taught universal atonement rooted in a universal love of God for all but also insisted that we may never say that Christ loves all men or died for all men—at

---

18 Ibid., 68.
19 Ibid., 83.

least not in a saving sense. What Murray meant by non-saving love and non-saving atonement, I do not know.

Certainly in his essay Murray never spoke of God's desire, intention, or purpose to save all men or mentioned the distinction *decretive* and *preceptive* in the will of God—a key distinction in the theology of the offer. But his language strongly suggested such a universal desire of God, and Murray's views immediately make one question whether he believed in a double will of God or rejected that notion.

"On July 7, 1944, a special meeting of the Presbytery of Philadelphia was held for the purpose of examining…Dr. Gordon H. Clark with a view to his licensure and ordination to the ministry. Against the fact that the meeting was called, as well as against its proceedings and decisions, a protest, or complaint," was directed to the Twelfth General Assembly of the Orthodox Presbyterian Church in May 1945.[20]

I am not concerned with all the aspects of Clark's case or with all the decisions regarding it.[21] What is of concern is that Clark was accused of denying the well-meant offer of salvation to the reprobate. The committee included the following paragraphs in its report and in defense of the doctrine of the well-meant offer:

> Such passages as Ezekiel 18:23 and 33:11 indicate that God not only delights in the repentance of the actually penitent but also has that benevolence towards the

---

20 Herman Hoeksema, "The Text of a Complaint," *Standard Bearer* 21, no. 8 (January 15, 1944): 174.

21 For a thorough analysis of the Clark case and the well-meant offer, see Herman Hoeksema, *The Clark-Van Til Controversy* (Hobbs, NM: Trinity Foundation, 1995). This book is a compilation of Hoeksema's editorials titled "The Text of a Complaint" that appeared in the *Standard Bearer* volumes 21 and 22 from January 15, 1944, through October 1, 1945.

wicked whereby He is pleased that they should repent. God not only delights in the penitent but is also moved by the riches of His goodness and mercy to desire the repentance and salvation of the impenitent and reprobate. To put this negatively, God does not take delight or pleasure in the death of the wicked. On the contrary, His delight is in mercy. God desires that the reprobate exercise that repentance which they will never exercise and desires for them the enjoyment of good they will never enjoy. And not only so, He desires the exercise of that which they are foreordained not to exercise, and He desires for them the enjoyment of good they are foreordained not to enjoy.

The question was: How can God make an offer of salvation to those who are foreordained to damnation? It does not explain the mystery of the co-existence of the full and free offer of salvation and foreordination to damnation to make the obviously necessary distinction between the outward call and the inward call. For even after full recognition is given to the truth that God effectually calls only the elect, the mystery of God's will in the offer of salvation to the reprobate still remains.

The Committee has no zeal for the word "paradox." But the Committee believes that great mystery surrounds this matter. Even the reprobate are the objects of divine benevolence, compassion and loving-kindness, not only in the gifts of this present life such as rain and sunshine, food and raiment, but also in the full and free overtures of God's grace in the gospel.[22]

---

22 "Report of the Committee appointed by the Twelfth General Assembly of the Orthodox Presbyterian Church to consider the Doctrinal Position of

The Thirteenth General Assembly appointed a special committee that included John Murray and Ned Stonehouse, both professors at Westminster Theological Seminary, to study the doctrines connected with the discussion of the complaint against the Presbytery of Philadelphia in the matter of the licensure and ordination of Dr. Gordon H. Clark.[23] Part of the committee report, which was submitted to the Fifteenth General Assembly, included a study by John Murray and Ned Stonehouse on the free offer of the gospel.[24] If Murray was confusing and unsatisfactory and left many questions unanswered in his essay, he clearly set forth in that study his views of the free offer.

Nothing was ever said regarding the relationship between the well-meant offer of the gospel and the atonement of Christ. While Murray discussed that in *The Atonement and the Free Offer of the Gospel*, the essay referred to earlier (written after this decision was taken), the Orthodox Presbyterian Church never officially entered into that issue.

There is probably a historical reason for this. The Christian Reformed Church made a decision concerning the well-meant

---

the Complaint of Certain Members of the Presbytery of Philadelphia," in *Minutes of the Thirteenth General Assembly of the Orthodox Presbyterian Church*, May 21–28, 1946 (Chestnut Hill, Philadelphia, PA: Westminster Theological Seminary, 1946), 38–68. The quoted paragraphs are found on pages 67–68.

23 Edmund P. Clowney, "The Thirteenth General Assembly of the Orthodox Presbyterian Church," *Presbyterian Guardian* 15, no. 11 (June 10, 1946): 172.

24 John Murray, *The Free Offer of the Gospel*, in *Collected Writings of John Murray*, vol. 4, *Studies in Theology, Reviews* (Edinburgh: Banner of Truth, 1982), 113–32. Because Ned B. Stonehouse contributed to the study resulting in this work, he is often listed as a coauthor. Because Professor Murray wrote the piece, it is included in his collected writings. As a doctrinal study commissioned by the Orthodox Presbyterian Church, the work was published as an appendix to *The Minutes of the Fifteenth General Assembly of the Orthodox Presbyterian Church, 1948*, 51–63.

offer in 1924, more than twenty years before the decisions of the Orthodox Presbyterian Church. No doubt the matter of the well-meant offer arose in the Orthodox Presbyterian Church because of the influence of Christian Reformed men who taught in Westminster Theological Seminary. Cornelius Van Til, R. B. Kuiper, and Ned B. Stonehouse brought the well-meant offer into the Orthodox Presbyterian Church and were instrumental in making it the view of many in it.

The relationship between the well-meant offer and the atonement of Christ was not specifically faced in the common grace controversy in the Christian Reformed Church. It was only after questions were repeatedly asked of the Christian Reformed men concerning the relationship between the offer and Christ's atonement on the cross that the topic finally attracted the attention of theologians in both denominations.

In the Christian Reformed Church the relationship between the offer and the atonement of Christ received official attention in the 1960s when Harold Dekker, in defense of the offer of the gospel and common grace, insisted that the atonement of Christ had to be general and for all men, except in its efficacy.

The doctrine of the well-meant offer received official sanction in the Reformed Presbyterian Church of North America (Covenanters) when it was made a part of their "Testimony" in 1980. In this document both common grace and the well-meant offer received official and creedal status. I quote from the Reformed Presbyterian Church's addition or "testimony" to chapter 10, "Of Effectual Calling," of the Westminster Confession of Faith:

> Preaching the gospel consists in the offer of salvation through Christ to sinners, accompanied with such an explanation of the various parts of God's Word as may

help to persuade men to receive Christ as Saviour, and to live and walk in him. 2 Cor. 5:20; Matt. 28:20; Isa. 55:1–3.

The elect are effectually called by means of the gospel offer. This offer is not a declaration to any sinner that his name is in the Book of Life. It is founded upon God's command to offer Christ and all his benefits to sinners. There is no inconsistency between the biblical doctrine of particular redemption and the command to offer the gospel to all men. Deut. 29:29; Mark 16:15; Luke 24:46–47; 2 Tim. 2:19.

We reject the teaching that the gospel offer of salvation is freely and truly offered only to the elect. *We reject* the teaching that particular redemption is to be so understood and presented that Christ as ransom and propitiation is not preached or offered to all men indiscriminately.[25]

Yet it must be added that this "testimony" does not speak of God's intention and desire to save all who hear the gospel. In this respect it is somewhat ambiguous.

The doctrine of the well-meant offer of the gospel—sometimes without official approval—has become all-pervasive within many Presbyterian denominations. Although some in these denominations oppose the well-meant offer, it is part of the preaching and teaching in these denominations and some have moved beyond it to outright Arminianism, a heresy that is an inevitable consequence.

It is worthwhile to include a sidelight to the history of the

---

25 Reformed Presbyterian Church of North America, *The Westminster Confession of Faith* (Adopted 1648) and *The Testimony of the Reformed Presbyterian Church of North America* (Adopted August 1980) in Parallel Columns (Pittsburgh: Board of Education and Publication, RPCNA, n.d.), 28–29.

well-meant offer of the gospel in Presbyterian thought. This sidelight concerns the controversies that plagued the Calvinistic churches in Wales during the seventeenth century and the first half of the eighteenth century. In a fascinating book, Owen Thomas recorded that history.[26] With an obvious bias toward those who taught a well-meant offer of the gospel, the author nevertheless demonstrated how the controversy over the extent of the atonement was related to and became the primary reason for teaching the doctrine of the well-meant offer.

While the churches in Wales were influenced by the Arminianism of John Wesley's revivals, Calvinism was also present among many theologians and preachers in Wales, due in large measure to the work of George Whitefield, a contemporary and co-worker of Wesley. Although the Calvinists held firmly to the truth that Christ died only for the elect, it was generally held by Calvinists and Arminians that Christ's atoning sacrifice was *sufficient* for the whole world but *efficient* only for the elect.[27] The subject of the sufficiency of the atonement became the core of the controversy.

The problem surfaced when the subjects of the sufficiency of the atonement and the preaching of the gospel were connected. The Synod of Dordt had spoken of the universal sufficiency of Christ's atonement,[28] connecting it not with the preaching of the gospel but with the Son of God who offered the sacrifice.[29]

---

26 Owen Thomas, *The Atonement Controversy in Welsh Theological Literature and Debate, 1707–1841*, trans. John Aaron (Edinburgh: Banner of Truth Trust, 2002).

27 Ibid., 151–52.

28 Canons of Dordt 2.3, in *Confessions and Church Order,* 163. "The death of the Son of God is the only and most perfect sacrifice and satisfaction for sin, is of infinite worth and value, abundantly sufficient to expiate the sins of the whole world."

29 Canons of Dordt 2.4, in ibid. "This death derives its infinite value and dignity from these considerations, because the person who submitted to it was not

In connecting the sufficiency of the atonement with the preaching, two errors resulted. First, on the grounds of the universal sufficiency of Christ's death, the gospel was made into a well-meant offer of the gospel. Second, the universal sufficiency of the atonement, as related to the well-meant offer, became not only a sufficiency for all men, but also a universal intention of God to save all men and a universal availability of salvation for all men.

John Roberts, a theologian in Wales, is quoted in Owen Thomas' book as teaching the following:

> Only with a view to Christ's death does God extend a sincere offer of eternal salvation to all sinners in general, in the gospel...The same relationship pertains between the blood of Christ and sinners in general as exists between the call of the gospel and sinners in general...
>
> Blessings are provided for sinners in general through the suffering of Christ.[30]

Thus bit by bit, the more Calvinistic theologians and preachers surrendered their views, overwhelmed by the argument that a universal sufficiency of Christ's sacrifice was crucial to maintain the responsibility of those who did not come to Christ, for without it one could not invite sinners to Christ or earnestly preach that the call of the gospel is God's invitation to accept what he earnestly desires. Those who held to the truth of

---

only really man and perfectly holy, but also the only begotten Son of God, of the same eternal and infinite essence with the Father and Holy Spirit."

30 John Roberts (1767–1834) wrote a work, originally in Welsh, entitled *A Humble Attempt at Explaining What We Are Taught in the Scriptures of Truth concerning the General and Particular Purposes of the Suffering of Jesus Christ* (Carmarthen, Wales: n.p., 1814). The quotations from this work are found in Thomas, *The Atonement Controversy*, 159–69.

scripture and the confessions that Christ died for his elect were branded as hyper-Calvinists, were said to be unable to address the gospel to unbelievers, and were censured for condemning as Arminian those who only disagreed on non-essential matters.

Thus Arminianism won out in the Calvinistic churches in Wales, and these churches remain Arminian—if not worse—until this day.

Chapter 8

EARLY DUTCH THEOLOGIANS

In this chapter I survey the views of the theologians after the Synod of Dordt until almost the end of the eighteenth century. Scanning the works of those great Dutch theologians, one concludes that it is difficult, if not impossible, to find the idea of the well-meant offer in any of their writings. Although they occasionally used the term *offer*, they did not mean to express God's desire and intention to save everyone who hears the gospel. Rather the theologians emphasized that the gospel is preached to many more than to the elect and that through the preaching Christ is widely proclaimed as the one through whom God has accomplished salvation, so that all who hear are confronted with the command to repent and believe and with the promise that believers will be saved.

Although there is no theology of a well-meant offer in the writings of early Dutch theologians, and their positive development of preaching and the call of the gospel contradicts a well-meant offer on God's part, yet in 1924 the Christian Reformed Church, in its decision approving common grace, defended the well-meant offer on the grounds that it had been taught by "Reformed writers of the golden age of Reformed theology."[1]

The development in the Netherlands of federal, or covenantal, theology had a bearing on the subject of preaching. In that development much attention was paid to the *promise* of the covenant, for the promise and the covenant are inseparably connected. This cannot be denied, for scripture often speaks of the two in the same connection. For example, in Genesis 17:7–8, the revelation of the covenant to Abraham is in the form of a promise. This is also found in Hebrews 6:13–20. Furthermore, the sacrament of baptism is a sign and seal of the covenant and the sacraments are added to the preaching to signify and seal unto God's people, through visible signs, the truth of the preaching. This means that the promise given in baptism is the same as the promise proclaimed in the preaching.

Although many Dutch theologians later interpreted the covenant as an agreement between God and man, with happy inconsistency they maintained that the promise is particular, that is, only for the elect.[2] As Dutch theology developed, the two ideas became inseparably intertwined.

---

1   *1924 Acts of Synod of the Christian Reformed Church*, 146.

2   The Protestant Reformed Churches repudiate the notion that the covenant is an agreement and believe that scripture emphatically teaches that the covenant is a bond of friendship and fellowship between God and his people in Christ. It is clear that when one makes the covenant an agreement, he is almost surely bound to the idea of a general promise. Under the idea of an agreement, all children receive the promise at baptism, but the promise becomes effective for them only when they become sufficiently mature to agree to the provisions of the agreement. For a detailed treatment of the particular promise, see Herman Hanko, *God's Everlasting Covenant of Grace* (Grand Rapids, MI: Reformed Free Publishing Association, 1988), 103–123.

Some theologians argued that the promise made in baptism expressed God's desire to save all the baptized children. Just as God's promise at baptism was considered to be general for all baptized children, so the preaching of the promise was considered to be an expression of God's desire and intent to save all who heard the preaching. And just as the theologians claimed that the promise made in baptism gave to all baptized children a certain claim to salvation (if they fulfilled the condition of faith), so it was also claimed that the preaching gave to everyone who heard it a certain objective claim to salvation (if by faith they accepted Christ offered in the preaching).

Many Dutch thinkers did not hold to the idea of a well-meant offer. However, as they continued to regard the covenant as both an agreement and a particular relationship with the elect, their commitment to the covenant as an agreement helped them gain acceptance of the idea of the well-meant offer of the gospel.

Quotations from some early post-Dordt thinkers will demonstrate that while they used the word *offer*, they meant something quite different by it from an expression of God's desire to save all who hear the preaching. While making some summary remarks and quoting from several theologians, Heinrich Heppe (1820–79) showed that preaching was considered to be a general proclamation of a *particular* gospel.[3] I include selected quotations in Heppe's *Reformed Dogmatics* from Johann Heinrich Heidegger (1633–98), Amandus Polanus von Polansdorf (1561–1610), and Johannes Cocceius (1603–69) regarding their views of the calling.

---

3 Heinrich Heppe, *Reformed Dogmatics Set Out and Illustrated from the Sources,* rev. and ed. Ernst Bizer, trans. G. T. Thomson (London: George Allen & Unwin, 1950; repr., Grand Rapids, MI: Baker Book House, 1978), 512–19.

3—This calling is imparted only to the elect; God not only has His word proclaimed to them through man (*vocatio externa* [*external call*]), but also introduces it by the H. Spirit into their hearts and there sets up living communion with Christ (*vocatio interna* [*internal call*]).—[Johann Heinrich] Heidegger [a Swiss theologian (1633–98)] (XXI, 8): "Calling is of those elect and redeemed through Christ. These alone are so called that they are also attracted and created new and begotten. They alone are those for whom God not only strikes their ears by His word preached through men, but also attacks their hearts, opening them, writing His law in them, changing them and inflaming them to love him."[4]

Heppe said that rather than the calling being described as an offer, it was considered a means God used to bring judgment on the unbelieving.

Heidegger (XXI, 9): "Clearly of another sort is the calling of those who are left non-elect and rejected. The non-elect called are not called according to the purpose and covenant of God, as heirs entered therein, but according to God's judgment and dispensation, whereby He suffers them in the outward communion of the elect through the Word of His goodness, convicts them of their wickedness, and cuts short their excuse for not coming to the wedding of the King's Son. Also they are not called so directly by God affecting, changing and regenerating the heart, as indirectly through men, who may strike their ears but cannot get through to their hearts. And so they are called by the Word preached

---

4   Ibid., 512.

by men; yet so that they are not brought by the Spirit of God to communion with God."[5]

In fact, according to Heppe, the notion of the offer was repudiated.

5.—Moreover outward Church calling is not imparted to the non-elect in such wise that God wished to present them with faith, should they refrain from resisting the activity of the H. Spirit. Otherwise the possibility would arise of a counsel of God being perhaps rendered futile by man. Besides it is to be noted that man can only resist the H. Spirit.—Heidegger (XXI, 10): "Nor does God altogether call particular reprobate in such wise that He has decreed and wills to give them faith and repentance just like the elect, provided only they do not resist the H. Spirit's call, as in the...(frivolity) of some. There are no decrees of God which men or any creature can frustrate. They are altogether effectual and have a most definite outcome. If He has decreed to give to some faith and repentance, He bestows them in time through the Word and the H. Spirit. In that case all men of themselves and by their nature resist the H. Spirit: Rom. 8:7 (the mind of the flesh is enmity against God; it is not subject to the law of God, neither indeed can be)."[6]

Heppe believed that the early post-Dordt theologians did not regard the outward call of the gospel as an offer in which God tells men he wants to save them. Rather they regarded the outward call as a call to salvation and a seriously meant

---

5   Ibid., 512–13.
6   Ibid., 513.

command of God to repent and believe, but the call is ineffectual in the godless because of sin.

13.—In the same way too it cannot be concluded that because the outward calling of the rejected is ineffectual, it is therefore not seriously meant by God. Outward calling is always *per se* a real calling to salvation, since everyone who follows it up thereby gains righteousness in Christ and eternal life: only, in the case of the godless, it is ineffectual because of their hardness of heart. Similarly, the calling from God's side is always seriously intended, since God promises grace even to the rejected upon condition of faith, and makes faith for them a duty. But of course God omits to give faith to the rejected, because He is not bound to do so in the case of any man.—Polan [Amandus Polanus (1568–1614), a German theologian prior to the Synod of Dordt] (VI, 32): "Ineffectual calling is of the reprobate…It is called ineffectual not *per se* but *per accidens,* not in respect of God who calls, but in respect of men who have deaf ears of the heart. In itself calling is always effectual, although it is not so in those who are perishing, as the sun is effective by his light in itself, although it by no means illumines the blind." From this it follows that even the calling of the godless is on God's side "sincere and serious." Heidegger (XXI, 11): "Whether the serious is opposed to a joke, God in no way plays in the business of calling; or to pretence, He likewise does not simulate, because He does not profess one thing outwardly in words, concealing something else inwardly in His mind, but declares to men by calling His plain, open and steadfast will. And since the parts of calling are commands and promises, as often as He calls He commands and orders them seriously to repent and believe. For He wills that they repent and believe by His preceptive and approving will, although He does not will by His discerning will, effectual to the giving of faith and repentance. He has the right to demand both...Moreover calling promises salvation, but not to anyone promiscuously or without condition, only to the believing and repentant person."

14.—Thus in the calling of the elect man's proclamation is essentially combined with the inward efficacy of the H. Spirit. Without this activity of the H. Spirit, who writes the Word in man's heart, God's Word itself is but an empty letter, slaying the sinner and enticing him into fresh service of sin.—Cocceius (*Summ. theol.* XLII, 13): "This calling takes place through the word heard Rom. 10:14f (how shall they call on him in whom they have not believed? and how shall they believe in him whom they have not heard? and how shall they hear without a preacher? and how shall they preach, except they be sent?)"—Heidegger (XXI, 21): "The outward calling of the elect through the word preached by men is very closely connected with inward accosting by the H. Spirit. Were it separate from this it would be of no avail. For the word preached by men strikes the ears of natural man, dead in sins...Any word, however divine, most true, most wise, most pleasant in itself and thoroughly lovable, when addressed to a sinner still dead in sin, whose heart has not been inscribed by the H. Spirit, remains but a letter, slays the sinner and provokes him to sin 2 Cor. 3:6 (...a new covenant; not of the letter, but of the spirit: for the letter killeth, but the spirit giveth life) Rom.

5:20 (the law came in beside, that trespass might abound;
but where sin abounded grace did abound more exceed-
ingly) [Rom.] 7:8 (sin, finding occasion, wrought in me
through the commandment all manner of coveting: for
apart from the law sin is dead)."[7]

Swiss theologian Johannes Wollebius (1586–1629) also
denied a well-meant offer. One cannot find in his writings any
reference to an offer in the sense of God's universal intention and
desire to save all who hear the gospel. Wollebius used the phrase
"Christ offered in the gospel," but he intended to convey that
Christ as crucified for sinners is presented in the preaching. Wollebius also spoke of faith as a "condition" to salvation, but he used
the term in the sense of making salvation particular. He used
"condition" not as meaning prerequisite but to impress his read-
ers with the truth that faith is the *way*, or *means*, of salvation only
for the elect. Wollebius referred to the common call of the gospel
as serious and for all, but he spoke of its purpose as being either
the salvation of the elect or the just damnation of the reprobate.

IV. The form of this calling consists partly of the offering
of the benefits of redemption, and partly in the injunc-
tion to accept it…

V. Its purpose is the glory of God and the salvation of the
elect. This is served both by the glory of his mercy toward
the elect who are responsive to the calling, and by the glory
of his justice toward the reprobate, who are disobedient.

VI. Therefore, this ordinary calling is primarily on
account of (*propter*) the elect, secondarily on account of
the reprobate.

---

7   Ibid., 517–18.

VII. He calls both (kinds of people) in earnest (*serio*) and without any deceit.

Concerning the elect there is no doubt. As to the reprobate, although they are not called "according to his purpose," or to salvation, nevertheless they are called in earnest, and salvation is offered them on condition of faith. Nor are they mocked because they have been deprived of the grace of believing. Rather, because they destroyed the original grace of their own accord, and also, by their evil passion, despised the means of grace, God therefore has the right to demand faith from them and uses it no less justly than do other creditors, so that their mouths are closed, they are without excuse, and the justice of God is upheld. Therefore, he does not call them to mock them, but in order to declare and reveal his justice.[8]

In his chapter 28, entitled "Special Calling," Wollebius explained his propositions II–XIII.

II. In the schools, it [special calling] is called actual election, effective calling, and internal calling.

It can be called actual election because by it God makes the decree of election effective. "Whom he predestined he also called" (Rom. 8:30). "I chose you out of the world" (John 15:19). It is called effective calling in contrast to the calling of the reprobate, which is not

---

8 Johannes Wollebius, *Compendium Theologiae Christianae*, chap. 20, IV–VII (Basel, 1626), quoted in John W. Beardslee III, ed. and trans., *Reformed Dogmatics: Seventeenth-Century Theology through the Writings of Wollebius, Voetius, and Turretin* (Grand Rapids, MI: Baker Book House, 1977), 116.

effective for their salvation on account of their own sin. It is called internal because the calling of the reprobate is only external, by the word; or, if they are to some extent enlightened and internally moved, the change is only temporary.

III. The principal efficient cause is God, the active cause is his free mercy, and the instrumental cause the ministry of the word...

IV. The "matter" or object of calling is elect man, who, however, is in himself wretched, animal, carnal, a sinner, separated from the life of God, altogether dead in sin. "And you he made alive, when you were dead in your trespasses and sins" (Eph. 2:1). "And you, who were dead in your sins, he has made alive" (Col. 2:13). "We ourselves were once foolish, disobedient, led astray, slaves to various passions and pleasures, passing our days in malice and envy, hated by men and hating one another" (Titus 3:3).

V. The semi-Pelagians, therefore, are wrong to attribute to man either a preparation for, or a tendency toward, receiving a call.

The reason is obvious in the words cited above, for just as no dead person can confer resurrection upon himself, neither can anything be attributed to man for his calling.

VI. However, man is not like a log in connection with his calling; he is a suitable subject for calling, since he is not a lion or a dog, but a rational creature. But man's reason, before it is enlightened, is worth nothing for calling.

VII. It is absurd to suppose that this grace of calling is extended to all, since not even that calling which we have considered above reaches all men, as the entire Old Testament record teaches; since, at that time, the gentiles were passed by and only the Jews were called.

VIII. The form of special calling is gracious action toward man, not only the enlightenment of the mind, but the changing of the heart of stone into flesh, or turning man to obedience.

This is clearly shown in the words above, especially Ezekiel 36:26.

IX. Therefore the Arminian innovators teach falsely when they say that the mind is simply endowed with knowledge and the desire is irresistibly awakened; that it is really up to the free will to believe or not believe, and the power of believing, but not actual faith [actus credendi], is given by irresistible grace.

This error is obviously contrary to what God says concerning changing the heart (Ezek. 36:26). And Christ also witnessed not only that the elect learn from God and hear him, but that all who have learned come to him (John 6:45).

X. The grace of calling is absolutely irresistible, not with respect to our corrupt nature, which is harder than stone, but with respect to the Holy Spirit, by whom his elect are so drawn that they inevitably follow.

XI. This act of drawing is not at all a matter of compulsion, or contrary to natural freedom of the will, which by its corrupt nature is prone only to evil, but which, when touched by the Holy Spirit, straightway follows willingly...

XII. The innovators (Arminians) are also wrong when they teach that sufficient grace is given to all men, although not the actual act of receiving and using grace.

This idea refutes itself. If one is not given grace of believing so far as actual faith is concerned, then the grace is not sufficient; for no one is saved unless he believes. We grant that common calling is enough to take away any excuse from the reprobate, although it is not enough for salvation. This is what God means in Isaiah 5:4: "What more could I do for my vineyard than I have done for it?"

XIII. The Pelagian teaching, that by the grace of calling natural powers are to be understood, is absurd.

Nowhere in Scripture is the word "grace" so used, but it means either grace that makes (man) acceptable to God, or grace that is freely given [*gratiam gratis*]: "To the praise of his glorious grace, by which he freely made us acceptable in his beloved" (Eph. 1:6). "Having then gifts that differ, according to the grace which is given to us" (Rom. 12:6).[9]

Those men were all contemporaries of the Synod of Dordt. Later theologians taught the same. Herman Witsius (1636–1708) essentially agreed with what has been quoted. He repudiated the views of Amyraut, expressed agreement with Turretin, and emphasized that the general call, in keeping with limited atonement, has as its purpose the salvation of the elect.[10]

---

9 Ibid., 157–60.
10 Herman Witsius, *The Economy of the Covenants between God and Man;*

Aegidius Francken (1676–1743) had some interesting remarks in his questions and answers regarding the offer.

Q 7. Does not God call all men by a sufficient grace?

A 7. By no means, for many are ignorant of the way of salvation, without which knowledge no one can be called to God's fellowship: "Who in times past suffered all nations to walk in their own ways" (Acts 14:16).

Q 11. Whereby does God call men externally?

A 11. By the word of the gospel, in which God offers to him Christ and all his benefits: "Whoso is simple, let him turn in hither: as for him that wanteth understanding, she saith to him, Come, eat of my bread, and drink of the wine which I have mingled. Forsake the foolish, and life; and go in the way of understanding" (Prov. 9:4–6).[11]

Although Francken used "offers" in the above quotation, in another question and answer he specifically repudiated today's idea of *offer.*

Q 18. Does God then intend the salvation of all whom he calls externally?

A 18. By no means. God intends only the salvation of the elect.

Comprehending a Complete Body of Divinity, trans. W. Crookshank (London: R. Baynes, 1822). See especially Book 3, Chapter 5, "Of Effectual Calling," 1:344–56.

11 Aegidius Francken, *Kern der Christelijke Leer: dat is de waarheden van de Hervormde godsdienst, eenvoudig voorgesteld, en ter oefening der ware Godzaligheid aangedrongen* [Essence of Christian doctrine, that is, the truths of the Reformed religion] (1713; repr., Groningen: R. Boerma, 1894), 243–44; my translation of the Dutch.

Q 19. Prove that God does not intend to save all through the external calling.

A 19. That would be in conflict with God's eternal decree of reprobation, in which he has determined to condemn some in their sins. He cannot intend to save those through the preaching of the gospel whom he has appointed as vessels of wrath.

Q 20. Does not God, then, deal dishonestly when he calls the reprobate to salvation, whose salvation he does not intend?

A 20. By no means; for in the calling God only makes known to the sinner the way of salvation, faith and conversion, and promises salvation only to those who believe and repent; in this God does not deal with them deceitfully, but only shows that he has made an inseparable bond between faith and salvation.[12]

This same emphasis is found in Peter Nahuys (1692–1766), a preacher in Monnikendam, the Netherlands.

Q. What do you understand by the external calling?

A. The external obligation [*nodiging*] that takes place only through the word to all who live under its proclamation, in which Christ Jesus and all his fullness is offered for naught.[13]

---

12 Ibid., 246; my translation of the Dutch.
13 Peter Nahuys, "The Calling in Particular" (lesson 11), in *Kort Begrip der Christelijke Leer: Verdedigd tegen Dwaalgeesten en Dwalingen* (1739; repr., Dordrecht: Abraham Blisse & Son, 1760), 187; my translation of the Dutch.

One cannot help but notice that Nahuys used "offered," although he emphatically asserted that Christ was offered "for naught."

When Nahuys explained "offered," he wrote,

Q. In the thirty-fourth lesson you state that there is a twofold calling—an external, or general, and an internal, or particular. With whom do we differ in that respect?

A. With the Pelagians and the defenders of common grace [*algemeene genade*. Notice that Nahuys repudiated common grace and included it with Pelagianism, but he recognized that common grace had always been inseparably connected to the well-meant offer.]. They recognize only a single moral calling, whereby they understand nothing more than a general invitation to all men without distinction, including a call to conversion and faith; by which invitation God would grant to all men without distinction a sufficient grace, whereby they, surrendering God's free will toward the good, can accept that calling voice of God and also convert themselves and become partakers of salvation.

Q. What is their basic error?

A. They want salvation as well as condemnation to depend on the free will of man.

Q. How do you contradict that contention?

A. Such a sufficient calling to all men conflicts not only with Acts 14:16, which says that God left the heathen to walk in their ways, but also with Matthew 13:11, where God grants his sufficient grace according to his good pleasure on some and withholds it from others. (Compare with 1 Cor. 4:7).

Q. However, what do you answer to this?

First objection: They say that if God would not grant sufficient grace along with the calling so they could heed that calling, God would appear to call in vain, which is not in harmony with his wisdom.

A. This objection rests on a false premise, as if when God calls all men externally, he does this with no other purpose than to save all of them, which we deny: "Many be called, but few chosen" (Matt. 20:16).

Second objection: But they insist on their point by saying, If God does not intend to save all those whom he calls, that external calling is only a mockery with man.

A. By no means is this true, for by the calling that man is most emphatically pointed to his calling; and thereby God shows his goodness to the man; while even the reprobate is the more convinced of his wickedness and rebellion.

Q. You also stated that the internal calling cannot be resisted. Who oppose this?

A. Once more, the common grace defenders, who maintain the opposite on a Pelagian basis.

Q. What do they have in mind with this?

A. Not only to have salvation depend on man and his free and indifferent will, whether for good or evil, but also to cast aside the more readily God's eternal and resolute will of gracious election.

Q. How would you oppose their position?

A. This stands not only in conflict with God's unchangeable and efficacious calling, but also with the harmony between man's obedience and the divine calling (Song of Sol. 1:4; John 6:45).

Q. How do they try to defend their mistaken notion?

First objection: They introduce Matthew 23:37 [a favorite passage of the defenders of the well-meant offer. Note what Nahuys said about it].

A. It is up to those parties still to prove that an efficacious and internal calling is spoken of in this passage. Even if we grant this, the passage still does not favor the wrong idea of these parties, for the Savior very clearly refers to Jerusalem and her children. They tried, were this possible, to prevent him from gathering the children. But in no way does Jesus complain about the children as if they have resisted that calling, which these parties try to prove from this passage. The opposite is true, for many did believe in him, regardless that this displeased and was contrary to the wishes of the rulers.

Second objection: The Savior nevertheless says of the Jews in Luke 7:30 that they rejected the counsel of God against themselves.

A. It is evident that this passage refers not to an internal, but to only an external calling, or invitation, which was done and presented by John the Baptist to their conversion, which invitation or demand of God, laid in the mouth of John, the Pharisees and scribes rejected.[14]

Clearer language could not be written. Nahuys expressly rejected as Pelagian any idea that through the preaching God intends

---

14 Ibid., 190–92; my translation of the Dutch.

to save all who hear. In this respect he reflected the teaching of those of his age.

Wilhelmus à Brakel (1635–1711) was another theologian of some repute during the early part of the post-Dordt period. One is convinced by his writings that he firmly held to the idea of a well-meant offer.[15] Nevertheless, he said the following about the calling:

> This begets another *question*: In calling the sinner to Christ, does God aim for the salvation of all? In calling all who are under the ministry of the gospel, is it God's objective that all would become partakers of salvation?
>
> *Answer*: No, for God cannot fail to achieve his objective. Then all who are called would, of necessity, have to be saved.

> To understand this matter correctly, the following should be considered:

> 1. The calling is first and foremost intended to gather in the elect…(Eph. 4:11–12). God does not send the gospel to those geographical regions where there are no elect to be found. Furthermore, when the elect in a certain region are gathered in, God generally removes the gospel from that area. Since the elect are in the world, however, and are intermingled with others, the calling comes to all; that is, to all the elect and also to others. By means of the calling, that is, by means of the proclamation of the

---

15 Wilhelmus à Brakel, *Hallelujah, ofte Lof des Heeren over het genadeverbond opgesteld* [Hallelujah, or the praises of the Lord relative to the covenant of grace] (Sneek: F. Hollkamp & Son, 1689).

gospel, God grants repentance and faith to His elect—
which He withholds from others.

2. We must make a distinction between *the objective of
God*—He who works—and *the objective of His work*—
the gospel. The very nature of the gospel is suited to
lead men unto salvation, as it sufficiently reveals to him
the way unto salvation and stirs him to be persuaded to
believe. The gospel is not to be blamed when all who
hear it are not saved; rather, man himself is the guilty
one. He is to be blamed if he does not desire to be taught
and led.

Such is the objective of the gospel. God's objective in
causing the gospel to be proclaimed to the nonelect is to
proclaim and acquaint man with the way of salvation,
to command man to enter this way, and to display his
goodness, presenting all the reasons to him for doing so
and promising him salvation upon repentance and true
faith in Christ. The Lord would indeed do this upon
man fulfilling the condition for which He holds him
accountable, and which the human nature, having been
created holy in Adam had been capable of doing. If he
does not accomplish this, it is not because God hinders
him or deprives him of the ability to do so, but because
man wills not; and thus man himself is to be blamed,
for it is the goodness of God which should lead him
to repentance. It is also God's objective *to convict man*
of his wickedness in his refusal to come upon such a
friendly invitation, as well as the righteousness of God in
punishing such rejecters of this offered salvation (John
15:20). Such is God's purpose or objective in allowing
the gospel to be proclaimed to the unconverted. It is,

however, neither God's purpose and objective to give to them his Holy Spirit nor to save them. This is evident for the following reasons:

First, it would be contradictory to the omniscience of God. God knows those who are His. He knows that the reprobate will not be saved, and it cannot be His purpose or objective to save them...

Secondly, it would be contradictory to eternal election. God has eternally chosen certain individuals by name and has appointed them to be the recipients of eternal salvation...

Thirdly, God cannot be thwarted in the achievement of his objective. He must of necessity accomplish what he has purposed, since he is omniscient, all-wise, and omnipotent...

Those who imagine that man, upon the proclamation of the gospel, has sufficient ability to repent and to believe in Christ...object to this...

Objection 1: God would act deceitfully if He were to call someone to salvation, and yet were not sincere in doing so.

Answer: God calls all who hear the gospel unto salvation, and it is His objective and intent to give salvation to all who truly believe. Faith and repentance are, however, singular gifts of God's grace, which He gives to all whom He wills to be saved. Others, however, God leaves to themselves...

Objection 2: God invites everyone to come to the wedding feast, that is, salvation (cf. Matt. 22:3–4; Luke 14:16). It must thus have been His objective that they would come.

Answer: ...The guest without a wedding garment could not be admitted to the wedding feast—not because he was not invited, but because by not having a wedding garment, he did not meet the condition included in the invitation...

Objection 3: If God does not purpose the salvation of all who are called by the Word, no one would be able to take it seriously, and no one would dare to come, since none would know whether he were addressed by God.

Answer: God's Word, being the truth, is sufficient for everyone. One may freely rely upon it, and one will not be deceived. That Word promises salvation to all who believe and to all who receive Christ unto justification and sanctification. This declaration is directed to everyone, and everyone must believe it, apply it to himself, and say, "If I believe and truly repent, I shall be saved." God does have foreknowledge as to who will be unwilling to come. God leaves man over to himself, doing him no injustice by withholding renewing grace from him who once had the ability to obey God in all things. God permits man to exercise his own free will, whereby he voluntarily rejects Christ and all heavenly benefits. However, God grants to the elect, in addition to His Word, the Holy Spirit, who bestows upon them faith and repentance. Since the required conditions are thus met in this way, they are saved.[16]

From the writings of those early post-Dordt theologians the

16 Wilhelmus à Brakel, *The Christian's Reasonable Service in which Divine Truths concerning the Covenant of Grace are Expounded, Defended against Opposing Parties, and Their Practice Advocated as well as the Administration of the Covenant in the Old and New Testaments*, trans. Bartel Elshout

155

conclusions are unmistakable. From the great Synod of Dordt through the late 1700s, no outstanding Dutch theologians held to the idea of a well-meant offer. Still it is repeatedly claimed by those who defend the error of the well-meant offer that their positions have a long and illustrious history.

(Ligonier, PA: Soli Deo Gloria, 1993), 2:205–8. The Dutch is found in *De Redelijke Godsdienst* (Leiden: D. Donner, 1893), 2:1893.

Chapter 9

LATER DUTCH
THEOLOGIANS

I f the Dutch theologians from the Synod of Dordt to the end of the eighteenth century did not hold to the present-day idea of the well-meant offer, how did this idea come into Dutch thinking and become such an accepted part of Reformed theology today? Several factors must be considered.

One element in this change in Dutch thought is undoubtedly that in the period following Dordt, the Dutch churches went into doctrinal and spiritual decline. The decline began almost immediately after the Synod of Dordt and increased in severity as the decades rolled by. With that doctrinal and spiritual decline, the great truths of Dordt, which strongly emphasized God's sovereign grace in salvation, were forgotten and even denied. This opened the door to many heresies, including a denial of the sovereignty of grace and an acceptance of the well-meant offer of the gospel.

Another element was the inroads of Amyraldism into English and continental thought. Amyraldism arose in France soon after the Synod of Dordt and introduced the error of hypothetical universalism, denied the sovereignty of God in election and reprobation, and taught a form of the well-meant offer. Those ideas also came into the Netherlands. While it was more than obvious that such errors would find their way across the border of France to its Dutch neighbor, the rise of the influence of Amyraldism was hurried along by the persecution of the Huguenots in France. During increasing pressure on the Huguenots, which came to a head with the revocation of the Edict of Nantes in 1685, many fled from France to find refuge in other countries. While most of the Huguenots were staunch Calvinists, some who fled were not, and they carried into other lands various heresies, including Amyraldism.

Diedrich Kromminga (1879–1947) wrote the following concerning the inroads of Amyraldism into the Netherlands:

> Before the revocation of the Edict of Nantes various heterodox opinions had made their appearance among the Reformed churches of France. At Saumur, Professor Moses Amyraud had taught a double decree of predestination, an anterior decree determining that Christ should make atonement for sinners and that sinners should be called to salvation, and a further particular decree of the election of some and the preterition of others. In 1649 he was cleared by synodical judgment... When the repression of the Reformed faith in France prompted the Netherlands to throw open its borders to the Huguenot refugees, the danger arose of the importation of these erroneous views...
>
> In the period of severe persecution that befell the Huguenot Church after the revocation of the Edict of Nantes, the purity of teaching did not improve among the persecuted...

These tendencies which were at work among the Huguenot refugees soon made their appearance also in the Netherlands and affected the course of scientific theology so that it began to lose its Reformed character.[1]

Various synods in France and the Lowlands warned against those errors. The Walloon synod warned against the view that "God's grace to sinners consists only in the preaching of the Gospel and not in a powerful operation of the Holy Spirit in the heart."[2] Heretics said that grace, which comes to all who hear, is not only in the external call, but also in the internal operations of the Spirit and is in the external call only in connection with the internal work of Christ's Spirit. That error inevitably led to the conception that salvation is dependent on man's will and that God's grace is resistible.

Nevertheless, certain Dutch theologians, influenced by Amyraldism, began to teach those views. Campegius Vitringa (1659–1722) and Herman Venema (1697–1787) taught a twofold decree of election, one general and conditional and the other particular and unconditional.[3]

Another factor that paved the way for the well-meant offer was the influence of wrong conceptions of the covenant. The covenant was defined as an agreement between God and man. That agreement—with its mutual stipulations, conditions, and promises—was put into effect when a man accepted the provisions of the covenant and made them his own. Because the promise of the covenant was signified and sealed in baptism,

---

1 D. H. Kromminga, *The Christian Reformed Tradition: From the Reformation till the Present* (Grand Rapids, MI: Wm. B. Eerdmans Publishing Company, 1943), 48–49.

2 Ibid., 48.

3 Ibid., 49.

and because all infants of believers were baptized, this promise was said to be made to all baptized children. Reprobate children as well as elect children were believed to have God's promise that he would be their God. While this promise did not become effective in their lives until they accepted the provisions of the covenant, in some sense all baptized children had a claim on the promise because in some sense God actually had made that baptismal promise to them.

It is not difficult to see how this is closely associated with the well-meant offer. The same promise signified and sealed in baptism is also proclaimed in the preaching. If the promise is made to all baptized children, the same promise proclaimed in the preaching comes to all who hear the gospel. Because that promise proclaims that God will be the God of those who hear, it quite naturally fits with the idea that the gospel is an offer in which God expresses his desire and intention to save all those who hear. In other words, a general and conditional promise of the covenant is fundamentally the same thing as a well-meant offer to all who hear.

This is not to say that everyone who held that the covenant was an agreement also held to the well-meant offer. There were many exceptions. However, such a view of the covenant allowed room for and influenced the development of the well-meant offer in Dutch Reformed thinking.

Another important factor in the development of the well-meant offer was the *Nadere Reformatie* (Later, Further, or Second Reformation). It is important to remember that the Dutch churches after the Synod of Dordt went into doctrinal and spiritual decline. This decline was characterized by dead orthodoxy that sapped the spiritual strength of the churches and was manifested in the lives of the people, so that under the influence of Dutch colonialism and economic prosperity, worldliness and carnality became endemic. That situation also prevailed in England and Scotland at the time of the Puritan reaction.

That reaction was important because Puritanism, which objected to the worldliness in the state churches, found its way into the Netherlands and was particularly attractive to church members who were concerned about the spiritual decline in the state churches. Puritanism came into the Netherlands not only by ministers, such as Augustus Comrie who visited the Netherlands from Scotland, and by ministers from the Netherlands who visited or studied in Scotland and England and returned to their own land, but also by Puritan writings, which were translated into Dutch and avidly read by those who saw in Puritanism a cure for spiritual lethargy and worldliness in the state church. The Puritans were fighting their own battles against the evils in the Scottish and English state churches. The writings of many Puritans were translated into Dutch, and the writings of Gilbert Ironside, Ralph and Ebenezer Erskine, and John Philpot were particularly popular. The Puritan conception of preaching was appealing because of its emphasis on the subjective life of the child of God. Insofar as those writers were followers of the Marrow men and taught the well-meant offer, the idea of the offer entered into Dutch thinking as well.

All those things brought about the *Nadere Reformatie* in the Netherlands, which was sometimes called Dutch Puritanism because of its similarity to English and Scottish Puritanism.

In this movement the first emphasis was on piety along the lines of Calvin in book 4 of his *Institutes*. In this respect it was analogous to the Second Reformation in Scotland. Gradually the *Nadere Reformatie* developed into a certain Anabaptism and mysticism and began to emphasize a definite content and style of life, the practice of godliness. With this practice came legalism, which spoke more often of the do's and don'ts of the

Christian life than of the liberty wherewith Christ has made us free. Those in the movement first practiced their mystical piety and devotion within the established church, but gradually they separated from the church and established conventicles. Then they separated institutionally under the leadership of Jean de Labadie (1610–74), Wilhelmus Schortinghuis (1700–50), and Friedrich Lampe (1683–1729).

The *Nadere Reformatie* received new life in the nineteenth century in the *Reveil* and the Secession (*Afscheiding*) of 1834. Because the *Nadere Reformatie* was influenced in part by English and Scottish Puritanism, and by that segment of Puritanism under the influence of the Marrow men, the well-meant offer was gradually introduced into Dutch theological thinking and became part of Dutch theology.[4]

The Secession of 1834, under the leadership of Hendrik de Cock (1801–42), Albertus Christiaan van Raalte (1811–76), Hendrik P. Scholte (1805–68), Anthony Brummelkamp (1811–88), and Simon van Velzen (1809–96), was a true reformation of the church of Christ in the Netherlands. The state church (*Hervormde Kerk*) had become so corrupt that it was becoming increasingly impossible for the people of God to survive spiritually within it. When the churches of the Secession were established, God was preserving his church and maintaining his cause in the Netherlands. The Secession was predominantly a movement among the common folk in the Netherlands, and it attracted many who were spiritual heirs of the *Nadere Reformatie*, that is, the deeply pious and religious Dutch folk who had been influenced by an unhealthy mysticism.

---

4 Joel R. Beeke, "The Dutch Second Reformation, Part 2," *The Banner of Truth* 57, no. 5 (May 1991), n122–23. See also Herman Hanko, *For Thy Truth's Sake: A Doctrinal History of the Protestant Reformed Churches* (Grandville, MI: Reformed Free Publishing Association, 2000), 8.

The following elements in the development of the well-meant offer among the men of the Secession and their successors are worthy of notice. There was no unanimity of opinion among the leaders of the Secession regarding the well-meant offer. There were two wings among those leaders; one was soundly Reformed according to the traditions of Dordt, and the other was less Reformed and more susceptible to error. The well-meant offer was an issue that separated the two wings. Hendrik Algra wrote that in the controversy among the men of the Secession over the preparation of ministers, Brummelkamp was under suspicion because the offer of salvation made his preaching too broad.[5] The idea of the well-meant offer prevailed among some in the Secession and was never officially condemned by the Secession churches. The result was that the view was commonly taught among certain segments, and it came into the United States when the people of the Secession immigrated.

The idea of the well-meant offer was closely bound up with the ground for the baptism of infants.[6] The promise of God, sealed in baptism, is also preached in the gospel. If the promise in the preaching is general, directed to all who hear it, the promise sealed in baptism is also general, made to all baptized infants.

The *Doleantie* (aggrieved ones), the second reform movement in the Dutch state church under the leadership of Abraham Kuyper, was quite different from the Secession. Thanks in part

---

5   H. Algra, *Het Wonder van de Negentiende Eeuw* [The wonder of the nineteenth century] (Kampen: J. H. Kok, 1965), 150–51. See also Lubbertus Oostendorp, *H. P. Scholte: Leader of the Secession of 1834 and Founder of Pella*, dissertation in English for the Free University of Amsterdam, 1964 (Franeker, Netherlands: T. Wever, 1964), 123–24 n16.

6   E. Smilde, *Een Eeuw van Strijd over Verbond en Doop* [A century of strife over the covenant and baptism] (Kampen: J. H. Kok, 1946), 24–25. See also Hanko, *For Thy Truth's Sake*, 10–15.

to the gifted leadership of Kuyper, the *Doleantie* was more church-politically organized and doctrinally articulate than the Secession. Kuyper was a theologian of great ability who left an indelible stamp on the church.

However, his doctrinal position was quite different from that of the Secession on some important points. The Secession was infralapsarian; Kuyper was supralapsarian. The Secession held to mediate regeneration; Kuyper maintained immediate regeneration. The Secession believed in temporal justification; Kuyper maintained eternal justification. Some of the men of the Secession held that the baptismal promise was general and conditional; Kuyper maintained that the promise of the covenant was always particular—only for the elect—and absolutely unconditional.

It is particularly my concern to examine Kuyper's views regarding common grace and the well-meant offer of the gospel.[7] In his early ministry Kuyper was a modernist, having been trained in the thoroughly modernistic seminaries of the state church. During his pastorate in Beesd, his first charge, he was converted and became a strong and ardent defender of the Reformed faith and of the doctrines of sovereign and particular grace.[8] Kuyper defended the truths of sovereign election

---

7   For many valuable quotations from Kuyper's writings and a careful analysis of his position, see Engelsma, *Hyper-Calvinism and the Call of the Gospel*, 173–92. See also Herman Hoeksema, *God's Goodness Always Particular*, 2nd ed. (Jenison, MI: Reformed Free Publishing Association, 2015), 58–62.

8   One can find those ideas throughout Kuyper's writings, including his major work on theology, *Dictaten Dogmatiek* [Dictated dogmatics] 2nd ed., 5 vols. (Grand Rapids, MI: Sevensma, n. d.). The teaching of Kuyper on sovereign and particular grace is beautifully set forth in his *Dat De Genade Particulier Is* [That God's grace is particular], originally published serially April 20, 1879, to June 13, 1880, in the Dutch periodical *De Heraut*

and reprobation, particular atonement, and irresistible and particular grace. He repudiated a Christ for all, grace for all in the preaching, a desire and intention of God to save everyone, and a double decree or twofold will of God so essential for the well-meant offer.

However, later in his life Kuyper began to teach common grace and wrote a three-volume work on the subject under the title *De Gemeene Gratie*.[9] It is not altogether clear why Kuyper changed his mind regarding common grace. Perhaps, as some say, Kuyper's modernistic education came through in his teachings in later life. It is probably correct, however, that he wrote *De Gemeene Gratie* when he aspired to and attained the position of prime minister of the Netherlands and that he developed the idea of general favor to justify his coalition with the Roman Catholics, which was necessary to give his Anti-Revolutionary Party a majority in the lower house of the Dutch parliament.

Although Kuyper taught common grace in his later years, his views of common grace were quite different from the views of common grace closely associated with the well-meant offer. *Algemeene genade*, or common grace, was used to denote grace that was part of the well-meant offer, but *gemeene gratie* was the common grace of which Kuyper wrote. *Algemeene genade* was said to be given by God to all men, including those within the church. It was somehow connected with the atoning sacrifice of Christ but was actually a blurring of the doctrine of election.

---

and soon afterward in *Uit Het Woord* book series (Amsterdam: Höveker & Wormser). The work in English translation is Abraham Kuyper, *Particular Grace: A Defense of God's Sovereignty in Salvation*, trans. Marvin Kamps (Grandville, MI: Reformed Free Publishing Association, 2001).

9   *De Gemeene Gratie* was originally published serially in *De Heraut* in the 1890s and afterward in three volumes (Amsterdam: Höveker & Wormser, 1902–4).

Kuyper viewed *gemeene gratie* as favor that God gives only to the wicked world, those outside the church and election, and independent of the cross. *Gemeene gratie* is manifested especially in the restraint of sin in the wicked world, so that men are rarely as bad as they would be without it, and it results in a natural, or civic, good that the unregenerate are able to perform and from which the people of God can benefit.

Kuyper insisted on distinguishing sharply between common grace and particular, saving grace. Therefore, he insisted that *gemeene gratie* operated outside the church and was not connected to the preaching of the gospel. Because of that definition of grace, Kuyper remained an opponent of the well-meant offer. With Kuyper there was no grace for all who hear the preaching, nor does God in any way through the preaching express love for all men, a compassion for all, a desire to save all, or a divine intention to bring all who hear the gospel to Christ and to salvation. Kuyper maintained his rejection of the offer for the rest of his life. Therefore, Kuyper cannot be appealed to in support of the well-meant offer, and his teachings on particular, sovereign grace remained his chief emphasis.

In 1924 the Christian Reformed Church in its three points of common grace married the two different views of common grace—*algemeene genade* and *gemeene gratie*. To understand how that came about, we must backtrack and recall the views of the well-meant offer held among the people of the Secession of 1834 who immigrated to America.

Their immigration to the United States began in the 1840s, shortly after the Secession, and some of the earliest settlers, under the leadership of Albertus van Raalte, settled in the area that is now known as Holland, Michigan. Soon after their arrival, and at the urging of Van Raalte, those settlers joined the Reformed Church of America, but soon many became disillusioned with that denomination and separated to form their own church, which became known as the Christian Reformed Church.

While those settlers were pious and godly saints, they were strongly under the influence of the thinking that prevailed among the leaders of the Secession. Insofar as the well-meant offer was taught among some of them, it was also taught in the early colonies. This is not to say that the sermons preached among them were not often soundly Reformed or that the truths of sovereign grace were not emphasized, but a strain of thinking that included the well-meant offer was there as well. As the Christian Reformed Church developed along those lines, the well-meant offer appeared more and more in the preaching. The doctrines of sovereign grace were heard less and less. The truths of sovereign election and reprobation were preached less and less. Increasingly the emphasis fell on Arminian views. As one reads the sermons printed during that period, he cannot help but be struck that the sharp emphasis on the truth of sovereign grace was not sounded from the pulpits as it ought to have been, but was replaced with an Arminian emphasis that included the well-meant offer of the gospel.

I quote from a few of these sermons to demonstrate this point. Dr. Clarence Bouma in a sermon on Luke 19:41–42 said,

> Jesus wept. In his weeping he is also the priest who reaches out his hands to those who are sinking away in order to save them yet.
>
> In that manner Jesus is the great high priest, who not only weeps but also in his weeping prays. He spreads out his arms to the apostate city and prays. Even as a mother extends her arms to her son as he leaves to go into the world and toward the abyss, whether perchance he may still rush into the safety of mother's arms.

How great and wide is his mercy! If thou had known this day. Jesus had preached peace at the former feasts. Now it is the last time; soon he will die. Now it is the eleventh hour; soon Jerusalem will be destroyed. *But even still at the eleventh hour Jesus stands there, praying for conversion for apostate Jerusalem. Even at the eleventh hour he stands at the closed door of the heart of the sinner. Frequently insulted and mocked, he still calls! Oh, if in this day you would recognize what pertains to your peace!* How great is his compassion. It reaches out even to Jerusalem...You also, even you. Many have already come to the fountain of life; you come also, Jerusalem. Many around the sinner already drank of those waters, maybe a pious father or a God-fearing mother. *Christ does not want anyone to go lost.* He therefore stands at the door of the strongly barred heart calling, "You come also; why should you perish?"[10]

In a sermon on Ephesians 5:2, Rev. J. Keizer, after speaking of the love of Christ for his own, concluded with a word of application:

Many walk no longer with us; they have turned their backs to God's covenant and words, even their heel, their neck, the cold shoulder. Their end is the way of death; as children of the kingdom they will perish. Return still, ye who are so averse; the Lord will still accept you. He waits to be gracious to you.[11]

10 Clarence Bouma, *Genade Geneest* [Healed by grace] (Wageningen: Gebr. Zomer & Keuning, n. d.), 102–4; my translation of the Dutch and emphasis. Bouma was a professor at Calvin seminary during the 1924 controversy on common grace.
11 J. Keizer, "De Liefde van Christus" [The love of Christ], in *Van De Onzen*

Those immigrants were clearly subjected to Arminian preaching in some instances. While generally pious folk, they were under the influence of Dutch Puritanism. Although the Reformed faith in many respects was preserved among them, they were also somewhat doctrinally weak.

It is evident from further developments that many among them held to common grace and to the well-meant offer of the gospel. Some maintained that common grace was closely connected with general revelation. Common grace supposedly conveyed to all men, apart from the gospel, a knowledge of God whereby all had some understanding of the truth, although imperfectly.

While the idea that God makes himself known in creation is certainly in keeping with what Paul teaches in Romans 1:18–32, that this general revelation is grace is a serious error and contrary to the text, which says that God's revelation is of his wrath, which is given so that the wicked are without excuse (vv. 18, 20). General revelation creates in man a yearning for God and a desire to know him more perfectly, and not only enables man to develop in science, philosophy, jurisprudence, and the like, but also prepares him for the gospel and serves as a point of contact in gospel preaching.

Bavinck wrote,[12]

The Christian, who sees everything in the light of the Word of God, is anything but narrow in his view. He is generous in heart and mind...He cannot let go his belief that the revelation of God in Christ, to which he

---

[From that which is ours] (Grand Rapids, MI: B. Sevensma, 1910), 19; my translation of the Dutch.

12 Dutch theologian Herman Bavinck was a child of the Secession of 1834. He retained that influence all his life. He wrote in the latter nineteenth and early twentieth centuries.

owes his life and salvation, has a special character. This belief does not exclude him from the world, but rather puts him in position to trace out the revelation of God in nature and history, and puts the means at his disposal by which he can recognize the true and the good and the beautiful and separate them from the false and sinful alloys of men.

So it is that he makes a distinction between a *general* and a *special* revelation of God. In the general revelation God makes use of the usual run of phenomena and the usual course of events; in the special revelation He often employs unusual means, appearances, prophecy, and miracles to make Himself known to man. The contents of the first kind are especially the attributes of power, wisdom, and goodness; those of the second kind are especially God's holiness and righteousness, compassion and grace. The first is directed to all men and, by means of common grace, serves to restrain the eruption of sin; the second comes to all those who live under the Gospel and has as its glory, by special grace, the forgiveness of sins and the renewal of life.

But, however essentially the two are to be distinguished, they are also intimately connected with each other...Grace is the content of both revelations, common in the first, special in the second, but in such a way that the one is indispensable for the other.

It is common grace which makes special grace possible, prepares the way for it, and later supports it; and special grace, in its turn, leads common grace up to its own level and puts it into its service. Both revelations, finally, have as their purpose the preservation of the human race, the first by sustaining it, and the second by redeeming it, and both in this way serve the end of glorifying all of God's excellences.[13]

William Masselink said that general revelation is brought about by a general and universal operation of the Spirit in the hearts of all men.[14] This view connects with the well-meant offer of the gospel. Masselink said that the basis for the general offer is the general external and internal revelation of the Holy Spirit that comes to all men. He said that general revelation witnesses within the souls of the ungodly as well as of the godly and is the basis for mission work.

So it was taught that if there is common grace shown to all men through general revelation there is also common grace in the preaching of the gospel. That is, the gospel itself is objective grace to all who hear. The gospel is evidence of God's favor to all who hear. That God even gives the gospel at all is evidence of his favor to all men. The idea of objective grace shown in the gospel was usually interpreted as *subjective* grace as well, for it is impossible to separate the objective and subjective elements of grace.

Thus the gospel objectively expresses God's desire and willingness to save all who hear, and thus he manifests his universal grace; but God also subjectively bestows grace through the preaching to all so they are able to accept or reject the offered grace.[15] All of this led to a view of general, or universal, atonement—a Christ for all.

---

13 Bavinck, *Our Reasonable Faith*, 37–38.

14 William Masselink, *General Revelation and Common Grace*, 84. He wrote after the Christian Reformed Church took the official decision on common grace in 1924. However, he said that he reflected thinking to years prior to 1924.

15 William Heyns, *Manual of Reformed Doctrine* (Grand Rapids, MI: Wm. B. Eerdmans Publishing Company, 1926), 195–201. Heyns was a child of the Secession. He taught at Calvin College and Seminary before and after the

Many immigrants who came to the United States were followers of the *Doleantie*. In 1892 in the Netherlands, the *Doleantie* churches under the leadership of Abraham Kuyper merged with the churches of the Secession into what became known as the *Gereformeerde Kerken* (Reformed churches). The immigrants to the United States from both groups and from the newly formed denomination generally joined the Christian Reformed Church.

In some respects the influence of Kuyper's followers was good, for he strongly emphasized the truths of sovereign grace. Some of his followers were doctrinally sound and aware and able to defend and define doctrine with clarity and precision. But along with the Kuyperians who came to the United States also came Kuyper's views on common grace. Those views were strongly represented by a segment in Calvin College in Grand Rapids, Michigan, where they found a mouthpiece in the magazine *Religion and Culture*. As the views of the Secession and *Doleantie* clashed, there was a considerable struggle within the Christian Reformed Church.

That controversy was carried into the doctrine of the covenant. The Kuyperian influence represented the view of a particular, unconditional promise of the covenant, even though Kuyper had also made presumptive regeneration the ground for infant baptism. The Secessionists traditionally held to a general, conditional promise of the covenant made to all baptized children. Under the influence of Heyns, the Secession view won out, and thus the way was prepared for acceptance of the well-meant offer of the gospel.

All that came to a head in the controversy of 1924, which involved a dispute over the well-meant offer of the gospel.

Christian Reformed Church adopted the three points in 1924, and he had great influence on subsequent thinking in that denomination.

Chapter 10

⟨≈⟩

THE 1924 CONTROVERSY
IN THE CHRISTIAN
REFORMED CHURCH

Although there were differences of opinion on common grace in the Christian Reformed Church, a discussion of the subject was ignited by what came to be known as the Janssen case.[1] Dr. Ralph Janssen was professor of Old Testament at Calvin seminary. He introduced higher critical views of scripture into his teachings. When he was forced to give an account of his views, he appealed to the doctrine of common grace in support of them. His views of common grace were chiefly those of Abraham Kuyper, and Janssen connected common grace to his higher critical views in various ways.[2] While Janssen never men-

---

1   Before the Janssen case, Herman Hoeksema had begun a criticism of Kuyperian common grace in the Christian Reformed Church's denominational magazine, the *Banner*, but it had aroused no discussion or controversy.

2   For a detailed examination of this, see Herman Hanko, *A Study of the Relation between the Views of Prof. R. Janssen and Common Grace* (Th.M. thesis, Calvin seminary, 1988).

tioned a well-meant offer in his writings, he brought the issue of common grace before the churches.

The Christian Reformed synod of 1922 condemned Janssen's higher critical views, but the synod did not make any decisions regarding common grace. That crucial matter, the basis for Janssen's defense, was left untouched. In a way this was sad, for the outcome of the common grace struggle might have been considerably different had the issue been tackled then. Many Janssen supporters remained in the church, although Janssen was dismissed from his position as professor. Because of the presence of those supporters in the Christian Reformed Church, nothing of the disagreements over common grace was really resolved by the decision against Janssen.

Herman Hoeksema was at that time minister in Eastern Avenue Christian Reformed Church in Grand Rapids, Michigan. Some in the denomination attacked Hoeksema for his denial of common grace.[3] This resulted in an exchange of books and pamphlets,[4] and strangely enough, a few protests from members of his congregation and others in the denomination. Those protests not only questioned Hoeksema's attacks on Kuyperian common grace, but they also challenged Hoeksema's position on

---

3   Hoeksema's early writings on the subject criticized especially Abraham Kuyper's view of common grace. Only after Janssen had appealed to common grace in defense of his position did Hoeksema more clearly develop his views.

4   See Henry Danhof and Herman Hoeksema, *Van Zonde en Genade* [Of sin and grace] (Kalamazoo, MI: Dalm Printing Co., n.d.). The English translation is Henry Danhof and Herman Hoeksema, *Sin and Grace*, ed. Herman Hanko, trans. Cornelius Hanko (Grandville, MI: Reformed Free Publishing Association, 2003). For a translation and compilation of the pamphlets, see Henry Danhof and Herman Hoeksema, *The Rock Whence We Are Hewn: God, Grace, and Covenant*, ed. David J. Engelsma (Jenison, MI: Reformed Free Publishing Association, 2015), 60–290.

the well-meant offer of the gospel. All that material eventually came to the Christian Reformed synod of 1924.[5] Synod made three doctrinal statements concerning the doctrine of common grace and the well-meant offer.

Concerning the first point, with regard to the favorable disposition of God toward mankind in general, and not only to the elect, Synod declares that according to the Scripture and the confessions it is determined that besides the saving grace of God, shown only to the elect unto eternal life, there is a certain kind of favor or grace of God which He shows to His creatures in general. This is evidenced by the quoted Scripture passages and from the Canons of Dort 2.5 and 3–4.8–9, which deals with the general offer of the Gospel; whereas the quoted declarations of Reformed writers from the golden age of Reformed theology also give evidence that our Reformed fathers from of old have advocated these opinions...

With respect to the second point concerning the restraint of sin in the life of individuals and in society, Synod declares that according to Scripture and the Confessions there is such a restraint of sin. This is evident from the quoted Scripture passages and from the Belgic Confession Art. 13 and 36, where we are taught that God through the general operation of His Spirit, without renewing the heart, restrains sin in its unbridled expression through which remains possible a societal relationship while from the quoted declarations of Reformed writers from the golden age of Reformed

---

5   For Hoeksema's protest against Classis Grand Rapids East to the Christian Reformed synod of 1924, see Danhof and Hoeksema, *The Rock Whence We Are Hewn*, 269–76.

theology it is evident that our Reformed fathers from of old have advocated these opinions...

Concerning the third point, in regard to the doing of so-called civil good by the unregenerate, Synod declares that according to Scripture and the confessions, the unregenerate, though unable to do any saving good (Canons of Dort 3–4.3) are able to do civil good. This is evident from the quoted Scriptures, and from the Canons of Dort 3–4.4 and the Belgic Confession Art. 36, where we are taught that God, without renewing the heart, exercises such influence on mankind that it is able to carry out civil good; while from the declarations of Reformed writers from the golden age of Reformed theology it is evident that our fathers from of old advocated this (same) opinion.[6]

A detailed analysis and criticism of the three points is not important here. I am concerned mainly about two matters: the teaching concerning the well-meant offer of the gospel and the relationship between the teaching of the well-meant offer and common grace.

The first point mentions the well-meant offer of the gospel somewhat in passing. The first point is confusing. It speaks of God's "favorable attitude toward mankind in general and not only toward the elect," which would eliminate the brute creation. But then, in a further elucidation, the first point speaks of a certain favor, or grace, of God that he shows to his creatures in general. So the entire creation is also the object of God's non-saving grace and favor.

That the grace of God is shown to the creation is also

6   1924 Acts of Synod of the Christian Reformed Church, 145–47.

evident from only one of the scriptural passages to which the synod referred: Psalm 145:9. If the synod had really meant that God loves his creation and looks in favor on it, no one would have disagreed. Psalm 145:9 proves that. Christ died for God's entire creation, and by his death reconciled the whole creation to himself (Col. 1:20). The creation waits for the full salvation of God's people (Rom. 8:19–22). The whole creation is to be glorified and made heavenly at the return of Christ. The meek will inherit the earth, which now belongs for the most part to the wicked.

Further, if the synod had said that God's goodness to mankind is revealed through rain and sunshine, as Matthew 5:44–45, Luke 6:35–36, and Acts 14:16–17 surely teach, no one would have objected. Who can argue with the fact that all God's gifts are good gifts? Does God give stones for bread or scorpions for fish? Can any gift of God be described as bad?

James certainly explained God's gifts when he wrote, "Every good gift and every perfect gift is from above, and cometh down from the Father of lights" (James 1:17). The question is not, are God's gifts to men good? The question is, are these good gifts tokens of God's favor? When that question is asked, two truths of scripture stand out. The first is that just because God's gifts are good, the wickedness of man in abusing them and using them for evil purposes is all the greater. Second, Asaph looked at the good gifts God gives the wicked from the viewpoint of God's purpose in giving them these gifts and concluded that with these good gifts God sets the wicked on slippery places that lead them to destruction (Ps. 73:17–19).

The well-meant offer of the gospel is mentioned only in passing in the first point: "This [God's favor, or grace] is evidenced by the quoted Scripture passages and from the Canons of Dort 2.5 and 3–4.5, 8–9, which deals with the general offer of the gospel." Almost all the scriptural passages and all the passages from the confessions to which the synod pointed refer to the well-meant offer of the gospel. Even though it is mentioned only in passing, it became the main point of the synod.

The second point speaks of a restraint of sin by the work of the Holy Spirit in the hearts of all men, which was said to be a part of God's universal attitude of favor. God shows his favor to all men, elect and reprobate, by giving his Spirit so that sin is restrained in them. While the connection between the well-meant offer and the restraint of sin in the heart of the unregenerate is not clearly set forth in the second point, the conclusion is obvious. The well-meant offer and the internal and subjective restraint of sin in the heart are both manifestations of the same grace of God. The idea is at least suggested that this grace that restrains sin is a kind of preparatory grace that makes one amenable to the gospel in which Christ is offered.

This is in keeping with what Bavinck taught. The internal and gracious operation of the Spirit puts every man in a position in which he is able to accept or reject the gospel.

The synod strengthened this idea in its third point, which specifically teaches that as a result of the restraining, though unsaving, influences of the Spirit, man is able to do good. Although synod specifically stated that this good is not spiritual but civic, the fact remains that it is still good in the sight of God. The idea that this good somehow makes man more susceptible to the gospel offer is implicit in the formulation of the three points.

These statements were aimed to lay to rest a controversy that had raged in the Christian Reformed Church between the Kuyperians in their view of common grace and the people of the *Afscheiding* and their views. In a clever way, these points of doctrine combined the two differing viewpoints into one doctrinal teaching, unfaithful to the genius of Kuyper, but satisfying to most in the denomination. The common grace (*gemeene gratie*) of Kuyper, which had nothing to do with the well-meant offer, and the general grace (*algemeene genade*) of the *Afscheiding* tradition were merged into one doctrinal statement.

While the synod spoke boldly of common grace as being the teaching of all Reformed theologians in the golden age of Reformed theology, it badly overstated itself. It offered no proof for that bold contention, and none can be found. The simple fact is that this view is not to be found anywhere in early Reformed theology; it is rather an innovation that must be traced back not to Dordt and John Calvin, but to Jacob Arminius and Moïse Amyraut. It is without question a serious and fundamental departure from the genius of the Reformed faith.

As the doctrine of common grace and the well-meant offer developed in the Christian Reformed Church, the Arminianism inherent in it soon came to clearer manifestation. Not only did free-will Arminianism begin to flourish in the Christian Reformed Church, but in the 1960s, Prof. Harold Dekker of Calvin seminary openly taught and wrote that the atonement of Christ was universal in its extent, availability, and intention, although he limited the efficacy of the atonement to the elect alone. He did this without ecclesiastical penalty and thus committed the Christian Reformed Church to an explicit universalism. Because Dekker said that the love of God was manifested in the cross, the saving love of God was universalized.

The errors of the well-meant offer of the gospel and common grace have serious consequences for the basic and fundamental doctrines of sovereign grace. The truths of total depravity, unconditional election, limited atonement, irresistible grace, and the perseverance of the saints (the five points of Calvinism) were not only seldom heard any longer, but also in many instances were openly denied.

Finally, because Hoeksema continued to deny those aberrations in the Reformed faith, he was ultimately deposed from office and put out of the Christian Reformed Church, even though the same synod that adopted the doctrinal statements testified of him that he was basically Reformed, but with a tendency toward one-sidedness.[7] It was this deposition and ultimate ouster that was the historic occasion for the beginning of the Protestant Reformed Churches.

---

7 Herman Hoeksema, *The Protestant Reformed Churches in America: Their Origin, Early History and Doctrine* (Grand Rapids, MI: First Protestant Reformed Church, 1936), 86.

Chapter 11

1953: The Conditional Covenant and the Well-Meant Offer

Although the well-meant offer largely ceased to be a debated subject in Europe of the twentieth century, this was less true in America. Even in North America, however, the well-meant offer was a dead issue in most denominations. For churches that under the influence of Charles Finney, John Wesley, Billy Graham, and others have allowed and promoted blatant Arminianism, the well-meant offer is not a matter of controversy or even a subject of debate. The well-meant offer is simply assumed to be true, and it is preached almost universally. Many churches, some historically evangelical, and virtually all liberal denominations have progressed far beyond Arminianism to outright modernism, for Arminianism is incipient modernism. Consequently they deny such cardinal truths as the doctrine of scripture, six-day creation, and all of the five points of Calvinism, and instead teach universal atonement or a health and wealth, feel-good gospel.

While in the last century the well-meant offer was not generally an issue in the ecclesiastical world, it continued to be such in some Reformed churches in America subsequent to the decisions of the Christian Reformed synod in 1924 regarding common grace and consequently the well-meant offer. The decisions taken by that synod were by no means the last word on common grace or the offer. The controversy was primarily between the Christian Reformed Church and the Protestant Reformed Churches in America, although other conservative churches undoubtedly kept a close eye on what was happening.

There is good reason that the well-meant offer continued to be a topic of controversy in Reformed circles. The reason is the antithesis—the sharp distinction between light and darkness, sin and grace, the truth and the lie. It is a biblical principle that where the gospel is most faithfully and strictly proclaimed, the forces of evil and apostasy are strongest in their contradiction of it. Where the truth is the sharpest, the lie is the strongest; where the lie is the strongest, the truth must be the sharpest. The history of the twentieth century is proof of this antithetical principle. In most churches there has been no disagreement regarding the well-meant offer because the truth was not preached, and the lie dominated unopposed. Exactly because the lie of common grace and its companion lie of the well-meant offer were contradicted by the truth of sovereign grace, mainly by the Protestant Reformed Churches, the debate continued from 1924 through the end of the century.

During the remainder of the 1920s and into the 1930s, articles pro and con (mostly con) filled the pages of the church papers, notably the *Standard Bearer*. Those articles, especially by Herman Hoeksema, detailed the error of the well-meant offer. Hoeksema even went so far as to make predictions as to the future results of the error of 1924, predictions that came true decades later. For a time there was unanimity in the Protestant Reformed Churches regarding the correct doctrine of the nature of the preaching of the gospel.

In the late 1930s this harmony began to be disrupted. The source can be traced at least in part to the association of the Protestant Reformed Churches with Klaas Schilder, professor at Kampen, the Netherlands, that began with his visit to America in 1939. Gertrude Hoeksema wrote,

> Toward the end of 1938 the possibility of having Dr. Schilder come to America to preach and to lecture was dreamed up by some influential Christian Reformed laymen. For by this time Dr. Schilder was a well-known scholar and author in the Reformed church world, and he was respected even though he was not agreed with on all questions.[1]

A conference was scheduled for March 29, 1939, in the Pantlind Hotel in Grand Rapids, Michigan, whence its moniker "the Pantlind Conference." The purpose was to attempt to reconcile the conflicting views regarding common grace, and consequently the nature of the preaching of the gospel, between the Christian Reformed Church and the Protestant Reformed Churches. This would theoretically pave the way for the potential reunification of the two denominations.

Although the Christian Reformed Church and the *Gereformeerde Kerken*, Schilder's church, were sister churches, the leaders of the Christian Reformed Church were very cool toward the conference. The conference was to consist of position papers by representatives of the two denominations, followed by

---

1 Gertrude Hoeksema, *Therefore Have I Spoken* (Grand Rapids, MI: Reformed Free Publishing Association, 1969), 242.

discussion. The ministers of the Christian Reformed Church, perhaps because they were leery of Schilder's possible opposition to their brand of common grace, stayed long enough to hear Herman Hoeksema's position paper.[2] Having not produced one of their own, with common consent they all began to make excuses, and one by one they gave flimsy reasons not to participate and left the conference. The attempt to resolve the issues of common grace and the well-meant offer was a complete failure. It is noteworthy that the Protestant Reformed Churches willingly participated in this attempted reconciliation, while the Christian Reformed Church obviously avoided participation. Thus the attempted resolution failed, and once again the battle was on.

The affinity between Schilder and Hoeksema, together with the Protestant Reformed Churches, was interrupted by World War II. After very little contact between the churches and Schilder during the war years, in 1947 Schilder came to the United States for a visit. Not long before Schilder came, Hoeksema was surprised to learn that during the interim Schilder had adopted the conditional Heynsian view of the covenant. The teaching of Heyns regarding the covenant was that of a pact with stipulations and conditions.

> The essence of the covenant is the promise in the sense of a conditional offer. On His part, God promises, that is, He offers to all who are born in the covenant that He will be their God, on condition that they also accept that promise of God and consent to the covenant. That conditional relationship in which God places Himself to the

---

2   See Hoeksema's position paper, "The Reunion of the Christian Reformed and Protestant Reformed Churches," in Danhof and Hoeksema, *The Rock Whence We Are Hewn*, 439–71.

seed of the covenant, the realization of which depends on the consent and acceptance of the covenant member—that is for Heyns the essence of the covenant.[3]

This brief summary of the history is significant not because it concerns primarily the well-meant offer. It does not. The controversy that led to the schism of 1953 in the Protestant Reformed Churches had to do first and foremost with the doctrine of the covenant. The debate centered on the conditional or unconditional nature of the covenant. The issue concerned the difference between the Arminian and the Reformed concepts of the covenant.

However, the error of the conditional covenant bled over into the content of the preaching. Hubert De Wolf, one of the pastors of First Protestant Reformed Church in Grand Rapids, Michigan, in a sermon on Luke 16:19–31, said, "God promises everyone of you that, if you believe, you will be saved."[4] Subsequently he made the further statement, "Our act of conversion is a prerequisite to enter into the kingdom."[5]

After much controversy and following numerous wranglings and church political maneuvers, the denomination was divided between those who wanted a conditional covenant and the well-meant offer and those who maintained the Reformed

---

3 Herman Hoeksema, *Believers and Their Seed: Children in the Covenant*, rev. ed. (Grandville, MI: Reformed Free Publishing Association, 1997), 16–17.

4 *Acts of Synod, Protestant Reformed Churches in America, 1954*, 54. See also Gertrude Hoeksema, *A Watered Garden: A Brief History of the Protestant Reformed Churches in America* (Grand Rapids, MI: Reformed Free Publishing Association, 1992), 177–78; David J. Engelsma, *Battle for Sovereign Grace in the Covenant: The Declaration of Principles* (Jenison, MI: Reformed Free Publishing Association, 2013), 24, 104.

5 *Acts of Synod, 1954*, 54. See also Hoeksema, *A Watered Garden*, 179; Engelsma, *Battle for Sovereign Grace in the Covenant*, 104.

view of the covenant and of the preaching. As events unfolded, it became clear that the schism of 1953 involved the issue of the well-meant offer in the preaching.

It must be clearly stated that the connection between the conditional covenant and the well-meant offer is historically only peripheral: the relationship between the two is not first and foremost historical, but theological and doctrinal. The relationship between the conditional covenant and the well-meant offer is such that the first necessitates the second. The well-meant offer, preached by those who caused the schism, was a doctrinal and practical consequence of their teaching of a conditional covenant.

This is not difficult to understand. If you say, "God promises every one of you that, if you believe, you will be saved," you are thereby preaching the well-meant offer: God wants to save you (in the context of the covenant), but you must believe and accept his promise before he can and will do so. Faith is a condition to salvation, and the preaching must demand that God's people fulfill the condition of faith in order to be saved. Thus the conditional covenant made possible—and even necessary—the well-meant offer. The question is whether faith is a condition for the realization of the covenant or whether it is a benefit of the covenant. If the latter is not true, then faith is a work of man. How can the covenant be conditioned on faith, while the gospel proclaims God's absolute sovereignty in the establishment, maintenance, and realization of the covenant? The two ideas are mutually exclusive.

That the well-meant offer played a part, however small, in the history detailed above is substantiated by the subsequent history. After trying but failing for a time to maintain their own denomination, those who held to the conditional covenant and the well-meant offer returned to the Christian Reformed Church, which without reservation taught both of these erroneous doctrines. History does not lie.

Chapter 12

THE DEKKER CASE

A t the end of 1962, just less than a decade after the schism of 1953 in the Protestant Reformed Churches, and immediately following the return of the schismatics to the Christian Reformed Church, the controversy regarding the twin issues of common grace and the well-meant offer erupted again. The occasion was two articles in the *Reformed Journal* by Harold Dekker, associate professor of missions at Calvin Theological Seminary in Grand Rapids, Michigan.

The thesis of the articles is that the well-meant offer requires universal atonement and that the well-meant offer can and must be proclaimed to all who come into contact with the preaching of the gospel. The articles are perhaps the clearest delineation of the well-meant offer that can be found.[1]

Two points are worthy of note by way of introduction to Dekker's writings and the response by many. One is that the controversy regarding common grace and the well-meant offer

---

1   Harold Dekker, "God So Loved—ALL Men!" *Reformed Journal* 12, no. 11 (December, 1962): 5–7; Harold Dekker, "God So Loved—ALL Men! (II)," *Reformed Journal* 13, no. 2 (February, 1963): 13–15.

arose in the context of missions. As professor of missions, Dekker raised the question, what must be preached on the mission field? The other is that the argumentation took place in the light of the three points of common grace adopted by the Christian Reformed Church in 1924 and in light of the issue whether the atonement is universal or limited. Although Dekker's views eventually became an official synodical matter, the debate was carried on primarily in a number of magazines in the public forum. Numerous positions, pro and con, were taken by a variety of influential individuals. Dekker began his writing with the following premise:

> The most basic and comprehensive of all missionary principles is the love of God. In divine love missions finds both its conception and its initiation...From God's love missions draws its motivation and its methodology.[2]

In the context of John 3:16 he wrote,

> Can an unlimited love be limited in its scope? Can an unrestricted love be restricted in those whom it loves? Can the infinite love of the incarnation have as its object only a part of mankind? Hardly. Neither does the Bible teach this. Rather we are told, "God so loved *the world* that he gave." Whether taken as the cosmos or as the human race, "world" in this passage clearly covers all men. By no strain of exegesis can God's redemptive love be confined to any special group. Neither the language of this verse nor the broadest context of Scripture will allow any other interpretation but that God loves all men.[3]

---

2 Dekker, "God So Loved—ALL Men!", 5.
3 Ibid.

He continued, "The universal love of God is also revealed in His invitation of the gospel, sincerely extended to all without reservation or limitation. Scripture gives numerous examples of God's universal and well-meant offer of the gospel (e.g., Isa. 45:22 and Matt. 11:28)."[4]

Here already Dekker's theological train had gone off the track, because the gospel is never an invitation or a well-meant offer, but the divine command to repent and believe. He compounded his error and at the same time strengthened his conception of the well-meant offer by asserting that it is not purely theoretical, but that

> God's sincere invitation of the gospel to all involves His desire that it be accepted by all. In a purely theoretical way it is possible to conceive of someone offering something to another without the desire that it be accepted. But the Scriptures allow no such casuistry in conceiving of God's offer of the gospel to all men.[5]

As proof for his contention, he cited Ezekiel 18:23, 33:11, 2 Peter 3:9, and 1 Timothy 2:1–4, historically among the Arminians' favorite proof texts.

Dekker continued and spoke of the love of God, which in his view stands behind and makes possible the well-meant offer. He characterized this love as universal:

> The universal love of God stands out in Scripture in bold beauty and unimpaired power. It is regrettable that some theologians, for the sake of a limited election, place limitation on the love of God. The most extreme and destructive form that this takes is the arbitrary

---

4   Ibid.
5   Ibid.

interpretation of words such as "world" as "elect world," and "all men" as "all elect men." This kind of limitation has neither hermeneutical nor dogmatical justification.[6]

Commenting on various passages that teach limited atonement, Dekker said, "They do affirm that Christ died for His sheep, His church, His people or the elect, but about the possibility that He may also have died for others these passages say nothing."[7] Here he committed the logical fallacy of the argument from silence. It is impossible to prove or disprove what does not exist. This error obviously vitiates his argument.

In speaking of the atonement, and consequently what the content of the preaching must be, Dekker distinguished four factors: sufficiency, availability, design, and efficacy. After asserting the universal sufficiency of the atonement, he asked, "Is the salvation which the atonement provided *available* to all men?" He answered, "Indeed it is. Otherwise the well-meant offer of the gospel is a farce, for it then offers sincerely to all men what cannot be sincerely said to be available to all."[8]

After stating that God desires the salvation of all as part of his design in the atonement, Dekker concluded: "The only point at which Scripture and the Reformed confessions point to a limited design in the atonement is at the point of *efficacy*. Only there can a doctrine of limited atonement be formulated which does not do clear violence to Biblical teaching concerning the universal love of God."[9]

Becoming more practical, Dekker wrote,

---

6   Ibid., 6.
7   Ibid.
8   Ibid., 7.
9   Ibid.

The doctrine of limited atonement as taught by Berkhof and others has commonly been used to place a taboo on the proposition that Christ died for all men and on any statement by a missionary to unbelievers such as, "Christ died for you." Supposedly such language is Arminian. Actually, it is not necessarily so…If the Church is unwilling to say in any sense that Christ died for all men and refuses to say to unbelievers, in addition to "God loves you," "Christ died for you," it places the infinite love of God under an illegitimate restriction.

The doctrine of limited atonement as commonly understood and observed in the Christian Reformed Church impairs the principle of the universal love of God and tends to inhibit missionary spirit and activity.[10]

Predictably Dekker's forthright teaching of universal atonement as the content of the well-meant offer provoked a storm of protest both from within and from outside the Christian Reformed Church. Two months after his original article, Dekker wrote another to answer his critics.

One man wrote that "the publication of [his] article was 'untimely…because of recent mergers with the Protestant Reformed brethren, who have just been through endless bickering and controversies.'"[11] Another asked, "Now is the term 'world' understood to mean 'not confined to any special group,' or is it understood to mean 'all men individually?'" to which Dekker replied, "My answer is the latter. I mean all men, person for person."[12]

---

10 Ibid.
11 Dekker, "God So Loved—ALL Men! (II)," 13.
12 Ibid, 14.

Immediately after the publication of Dekker's first article, Herman Hoeksema reacted to his views regarding universal atonement and the well-meant offer by calling them "rank Arminianism":

I certainly do not agree with Prof. Dekker. His views are, as I have expressed in the heading above these articles, rank Arminianism. But if I were in his shoes and a case were made against me, I would surely appeal to the *Three Points* as explained by Berkhof and also by H. J. Kuiper, in order to prove that I was in full agreement with the officially declared doctrine of the Christian Reformed Church...I repeat that Prof. Dekker can always appeal for his stand to the First Point of 1924. Do not forget that one of the grounds which the Synod of 1924 adduced in support of the First Point or in support of the expression that "there is a certain favor or grace of God which he shows to his creatures in general" is the general offer of the gospel.[13]

According to Dekker, he and Hoeksema were in basic agreement:

In Rev. H. Hoeksema's cogent and convincing analysis of my article, he says, "The first point of 1924 declares that God is gracious to all men, even in the preaching of the gospel; Prof. Dekker emphasizes that God loves all men. But what is the difference? Essentially it is the same thing." I am inclined to agree with Rev. H. Hoeksema in this judgment and to accept its implications.[14]

---

13 Herman Hoeksema, "Rank Arminianism in Calvin Seminary," *Standard Bearer* 39, no. 10 (February 15, 1963): 220.

14 Dekker, "God So Loved—ALL Men! (II)," 15.

Nor, according to Dekker, was there room for compromise: "Rev. H. Hoeksema is quite right, as I see it, when he suggests that essentially there is no tenable middle ground between his established position, i.e., that God loves only the elect, and the position I have attempted to set forth, i.e., that God loves all men."[15]

There was no lack of clarity regarding the differing positions of Dekker and Hoeksema concerning the love of God and the well-meant offer. Lest there be any misunderstanding, Dekker made his position unmistakably and unequivocally clear:

Let each one then who wishes to take a clear-cut position on the love of God and missions answer unequivocally whether he understands the love of God as taught in John 3:16 to embrace all men or not. If he answers yes, I believe that he is essentially in agreement with the position I have taken. If he answers no, I believe that he is essentially identified either with the position of Rev. H. Hoeksema, or with the position of those who hold to two loves in God (redemptive and non-redemptive).[16]

However, Dekker could not fully explain his position in light of scripture and the confessions, and thus resorted to the time-worn excuse of paradox:

Of course, no matter how we understand all of these matters, mystery remains. Can we explain that God loves all men while not all men are saved? Surely not. But is there anything that we really can explain about the love of God? Let us carry out our mission to all men according to the plain Biblical givens, leaving the

---

15 Ibid, 16.

16 Harold Dekker, "God's Love to Sinners—One or Two?" *Reformed Journal* 13, no. 3 (March, 1963): 14.

unexplainable where it belongs—in the infinite mystery of the heart of Him who is Himself love. The ultimate mystery for missions is the mystery of divine love.[17]

Soon James Daane, a Christian Reformed minister and assistant editor of *Christianity Today*, stepped forward in Harold Dekker's defense. While much of what he wrote concerned the nature of God's love and grace and therefore is not directly relevant to the subject at hand, Daane connected universal atonement and the well-meant offer.

He indicated that he was prompted to enter the discussion because the 1964 synod of the Christian Reformed Church appointed a study committee, because the churches were uncertain whether Dekker's position violated the doctrine of limited atonement. The mandate of that committee was "to study in the light of Scripture and the Creeds the doctrine of limited atonement as it relates to the love of God," to study "the doctrinal expressions of Professor H. Dekker," and to study "other related questions which may arise in the course of their study."[18]

The synod could have saved itself a great deal of time and effort if it had affirmed the doctrine of limited atonement on the basis of scripture and the confessions and condemned the heresy of Dekker, in which instance any secondary questions would have fallen away. But the synod decided to study the matter.

Daane immediately and correctly connected 1924 and 1964. He pointed out that for forty years, on the basis of the first point of 1924, it was rarely asserted in Christian Reformed writing and preaching that God loves all men and that this is the content of the well-meant offer. He commented approvingly, "Today, forty

17 Dekker, "God So Loved—ALL Men! (II)," 16.
18 James Daane, "From 1924 to 1964," *Reformed Journal* 14, no. 8 (October, 1964): 7–8.

years later, Professor Dekker is extending the theology of 1924, asserting that God loves all men."[19]

Speaking of the uneasiness in the Christian Reformed Church regarding the doctrine of two graces (saving and common) formulated in 1924, he attributed this to the fact that "the Synod of 1924 adduced the well-meant offer of salvation that comes in the preaching of the gospel, not only as a mere proof, but as an *instance* of common grace. It was against this that the Rev. Herman Hoeksema registered his strongest exception and leveled the charge of Arminianism."[20]

In summarizing the relationship between 1924 and 1964 concerning the well-meant offer, Daane rightly explained:

> The synod of 1924 quite clearly implies two qualitatively different kinds of grace. But it *also* teaches most explicitly that common, non-saving grace comes to the non-elect *in and through* the preaching of the well-meant offer of the gospel. I asserted that this fact was its proof for common grace, one given in the Scriptures and in the Reformed Confessions. As 1924 taught that common grace comes to the non-elect through the preaching of the gospel, Professor Dekker is asserting that God's common love for all men is revealed in and through the death of Christ. At this crucial point, then, there is no difference between the teaching of 1924 and that of Professor Dekker. There is no difference simply because what 1924 says comes through the preaching of the gospel, Professor Dekker says is declared in the Cross of Christ. And surely there is no essential and

---

19 Ibid., 7–8.
20 James Daane, "A Road Forty Years Long," *Reformed Journal* 14, no. 9 (November, 1964): 14.

qualitative difference between what is preached in the gospel and what is proclaimed in the Cross.[21]

While the debate continued in the religious press, the synodical study committee appointed in 1964 was working. However, after two years of labor, and after writing a seventy-page report, the committee was not prepared to come to the synod of 1966 with its recommendations. The synod avoided a showdown on the issue by recommitting their report to the study committee for further development and improvement. Among the related problems mentioned in synod's 1964 mandate that needed clarification and precise statement was the sincere offer of the gospel.[22]

The 1967 synod again took up the Dekker case. The motion that confronted it in effect declared Dekker's teachings to be contrary to scripture and the confessions. After twice failing to pass this motion, the synod finally reached an agreement. By an overwhelming majority the following decision was taken:

That Synod admonish Prof. Dekker for the ambiguous and abstract way in which he has used statements [concerning the love of God and the atonement.

Grounds:

a. His writings have resulted in considerable misunderstanding and confusion within the churches concerning the doctrine of the atonement.

---

21 James Daane, "Another Look at Common Grace," *Reformed Journal* 15, no. 2 (February 1965): 19.
22 Homer C. Hoeksema, "Op De Lange Baan Geschoven" [Shoved onto an endless path], *Standard Bearer* 42, no. 19 (August 1, 1966): 437–38.

b. His presentation of his views has resulted in widespread uncertainty concerning his adherence to the creeds.][23]

The decision was nothing short of amazing in its irrelevance and inaccuracy. After thousands of trees had become paper and oceans of ink were spilled, Dekker is "ambiguous and abstract"? Many adjectives could be used to describe him in his writings—clear, definite, precise, unapologetic, concrete, specific, understandable, lucid—but never ambiguous or abstract. How his writings on the atonement and the well-meant offer could result in misunderstanding and confusion is incomprehensible. Dekker taught universal atonement, plain and simple, and did so in the context of the well-meant offer specifically on the mission field. How there could be widespread confusion about his adherence to the creeds is equally inconceivable: he denied the clear teaching of the Reformed confessions.

The results were that since his views were not condemned, Dekker was free to teach universal atonement without ecclesiastical sanction, and that preaching of universal atonement became acceptable in the Christian Reformed Church. The result was also that the decisions of the 1924 synod were reaffirmed and validated. Dekker broke no new ground; all he correctly did was to carry the three points of common grace to their logical and necessary conclusion, grounding his doctrine of universal atonement in the doctrine of the well-meant offer: the well-meant offer became the occasion and rationale for the doctrine of universal atonement. Without repudiating 1924, the

---

23 *Acts of Synod 1967 of the Christian Reformed Church* (Grand Rapids, MI: Christian Reformed Publishing House, 1967), 733. See also Homer C. Hoeksema, "TRAGIC!" *Standard Bearer* 43, no. 21 (September 15, 1967): 484–85.

CORRUPTING THE WORD OF GOD

1967 synod did not have a leg on which to stand and therefore took a decision that was in reality no decision at all.

It is worth noting that the doctrines of common grace, universal atonement, and the well-meant offer are interwoven. This illustrates that the truth of the scriptures is a unity. If one doctrine is touched, other related doctrines are affected. The Dekker case essentially began with the question, what must we preach on the mission field? The answer was that unless the well-meant offer is preached, missions are either difficult or impossible. In order to justify a well-meant offer of salvation to all, the doctrine concerning the nature of grace needed to be adjusted from saving to common. Then only the pesky problem of the nature of the atonement remained: how is it possible to say to everyone, "God loves you" if the atonement is not universal? Thus touching one aspect of the truth destroys the entire truth.

Chapter 13

⟞⟝

RECENT
DEVELOPMENTS

Since the early part of the twentieth century when the Christian Reformed Church at its synod of 1924 made decisions concerning common grace and the well-meant offer of the gospel, the doctrine of the well-meant offer has been accepted almost everywhere in the ecclesiastical world. Although here and there a voice of protest against the heresy has been made, most of what has been written supports it. Many times those defenses of the well-meant offer have included attacks against the position of the Protestant Reformed Churches and the slanderous charge that those churches are guilty of hyper-Calvinism because of their denial of the well-meant offer.

That the teaching of the well-meant offer of the gospel has become so prevalent does not mean that in every case it has been adopted officially by broader assemblies of Reformed and Presbyterian churches. Frequently the doctrine is taught in the seminaries, preached by ministers and taught by leaders in churches, and accepted without question.

The doctrinal climate within many churches makes this

possible. Not a great deal of knowledge of and concern for doctrine can be found there. Insofar as doctrinal knowledge and concern are still found, the thinking of many is formed and shaped by man-centered theology, which is more concerned with preaching that appeals to man than with the glory of God. God's truth has fallen by the wayside.

Nevertheless, some developments concerning the well-meant offer of the gospel in some Presbyterian and Reformed churches can be found. There are many Presbyterian denominations in the British Isles, particularly in Scotland and Ireland. Of these Presbyterian churches, the most conservative are the Free Church of Scotland (Continuing), the Free Presbyterian Church of Scotland, and the Reformed Presbyterian Church of Ireland.

The Banner of Truth Trust, an independent organization that represents a wide spectrum of conservative Reformed Presbyterian and Baptist churches, is influential in the British Isles and throughout the world. The organization is noted for its publication of Puritan works and commitment to the promotion of the well-meant offer. The *Banner of Truth*, its magazine, regularly includes articles defending the well-meant offer of the gospel and criticizing those who repudiate it.

While the Free Church of Scotland does not have an official stand regarding the well-meant offer, it consciously stands in the tradition of the Marrow men, having its spiritual roots in that movement. Its commitment to the well-meant offer is evident from the fact that Donald Macleod, professor of systematic theology at the theological college of the Free Church of Scotland in Edinburgh from 1978 to 2011, wrote *Behold Your God*, in which he defended the well-meant offer of the gospel.[1]

---

1   Donald Macleod, *Behold Your God* (Fearn, Scotland: Christian Focus Publications, 1990), 123, 128–31. The book examines and attempts to refute

In its defense of the well-meant offer, the Banner of Truth Trust has published an edition of Arthur Pink's book *The Sovereignty of God*, in which every reference to the doctrine of reprobation has been excised.[2]

David Silversides, a pastor in the Reformed Presbyterian Church of Ireland, is an ardent defender of the well-meant offer. While his church as a whole has not taken an official position regarding the well-meant offer of the gospel, his open preaching and teaching of the doctrine has gone without reproof.[3]

Iain H. Murray, an influential theologian in the British Isles and an ardent defender of the well-meant offer, enlists the late Baptist preacher Charles Spurgeon in his battle against hyper-Calvinism to help him defend the well-meant offer.[4]

---

the Protestant Reformed Churches' objections to common grace and the well-meant offer.

2 Ronald Hanko, "The Forgotten Pink," *British Reformed Journal*, no. 17 (January–March 1997): 1–24. The article contains two appendices, "The Forgotten Spurgeon" (19) and "The Banner Edition of Pink's 'Sovereignty of God'" (20–24). This includes a sample of how the Banner of Truth Trust mutilated Arthur Pink's *The Sovereignty of God*. This article was reprinted with the same title in the *Protestant Reformed Theological Journal* 33, no. 1 (November 1999): 2–44. The reprint contains one additional appendix, "A Response from *The Banner*" (25–26). This was answered by Ronald Hanko in the *British Reformed Journal*, no. 25 (January–March 1999): 1–7, under the title "Edited Half Away: Some Further Considerations over the Banner of Truth Edition of Pink's *Sovereignty of God*."

3 David Silversides, "The Doctrine of Conversion in the Westminster Standards with Special Reference to the Theology of Herman Hoeksema," *Reformed Theological Journal* 9 (November 1993): 62–84. This journal is edited for the faculty of the Reformed Theological College of the Reformed Presbyterian Church of Ireland. The substance of the paper was presented at a 1993 Ministers' Conference of the Reformed Presbyterian Church of Ireland.

4 Iain H. Murray, *Spurgeon v. Hyper-Calvinism: The Battle for Gospel Preaching* (Edinburgh: Banner of Truth Trust, 1995), 66–99. A reply to the charges made in Murray's book is Hugh L. Williams' review, "Not So Sure

Erroll Hulse, another influential minister in the United Kingdom, has written a book on the well-meant offer in which he vigorously defends the doctrine. According to K. W. Stebbins, another author who defends the well-meant offer,

> He [Hulse] maintains that God "desires" and "wishes" the salvation of all...
>
> Concerning a distinction in the will of God, Hulse will only assert that "the Scriptures indicate that we are obliged to distinguish carefully between God's revealed will and His decretive or secret will..." If we ask, "If God desires, yes, wills all men to be saved, why are they not saved?" we can only answer, "Why should God do anything benevolent for those who curse Him?" He is not obligated.[5]

The Covenant Protestant Reformed Church in Ballymena, Northern Ireland, a sister church of the Protestant Reformed Churches, takes a strong stand against the well-meant offer. Its voice is heard throughout the British Isles and beyond, and it serves as a rallying point for all those who hold to the truth of the sovereignty of God in salvation. Other than that lone voice,

---

with Mr. Spurgeon, or Open the Mouth and Swallow It at Once: Being a Critique of Some Unfortunate Exegesis," *British Reformed Journal*, no. 14 (April–June 1996): 41–48.

5 K. W. Stebbins, *Christ Freely Offered: A Discussion of the General Offer of Salvation in the Light of Particular Atonement* (Strathpine, North Australia: Covenanter Press, 1978), 39. Stebbins is a minister in the Presbyterian Reformed Church of Australia who vigorously defends the doctrine of the well-meant offer and launches a lengthy attack against the position of the Protestant Reformed Churches as well as against the position of the Evangelical Presbyterian Church of Australia, which has officially repudiated the well-meant gospel offer.

however, few in the British Isles oppose the pernicious doctrine of the well-meant offer.

The same promotion of the well-meant offer is generally found in the United States as in Britain. The doctrine is accepted almost without question in most conservative Presbyterian and Reformed churches.

Many churches that have allowed the Arminianism of John Wesley and Charles Finney into their pulpits have become thoroughly modern and no longer bother with the controversy over the well-meant offer. They have moved beyond that error into others. This is not surprising because Arminianism is the germ of modernism. The Christian Reformed Church, for example, has long ago ceased to concern itself with matters involved in the well-meant offer of the gospel. Rather, it has become so completely universalistic that the particularity and sovereignty of grace are scarcely recognized. Graver errors, such as the denial of scripture's infallibility, theistic evolutionism, and the teaching of universal atonement have become widespread in its ranks.

In the late decades of the twentieth century the United Reformed Church was formed in an effort to combat and correct basic errors in the Christian Reformed Church. The reform movement had a golden opportunity to reject the errors of common grace and the Arminian well-meant offer, which lay at the root of the apostasy and the abuses that movement sought to correct. Had that reform movement done so, the fundamental errors that resulted in practical abuses would have been rejected, and the practical issues would have been eliminated on the basis of correct doctrine. Unfortunately this path was not followed. The result is that by default the United Reformed Church still officially holds to common grace and the well-meant offer. Had the United Reformed daughter of the mother Christian Reformed Church rejected these two fundamental errors, the outcome would perhaps have been different from what it was. Perhaps the issue of the well-meant offer, in connection with common grace, could have been considered moot on the basis of the decisions taken by the 1924 Christian Reformed synod. This, however, was not the case.

While many in Reformed and Presbyterian churches have attempted to hold to a well-meant offer of the gospel and the biblical and confessional doctrines of election and reprobation, it has proved impossible consistently to hold contradictory doctrines. The result was, not unexpectedly, that election and reprobation fell wounded and bleeding by the wayside. Reprobation is not preached; it is no longer believed. It is a doctrine that is lost in most Reformed churches.

The widespread acceptance of the error of the well-meant offer of the gospel is to be ascribed to Arminianism's gaining a foothold in the thinking of most churches. Arminianism has replaced the strong and sturdy emphasis on God's absolute sovereignty that characterized the thinking of Augustine, all the reformers, and countless theologians since the Reformation, and that was incorporated in the historic creeds of Reformed and Presbyterian churches.

If one would inquire into why Arminianism has so successfully replaced a strong and consistent emphasis on the absolute sovereignty of God, he can find the answer in man's sinful heart. God's sovereignty is destructive of man's pride. God's sovereignty smashes pride and puts man in the dust, so that he cries out with Job, "I abhor myself, and repent in dust and ashes" (Job 42:6). God's sovereignty humbles man because it puts man's salvation exclusively in God's hands and says to the sinner, "You are able to do no good at all; you are worthy of nothing else than eternal death in hell. If I am eternally pleased to save you by my grace, I will surely do so. But then your salvation is by grace alone. I will take all glory to myself."

Man will not permit himself to be so shattered, so he wraps himself in the tattered and useless robes of his own goodness and constructs a theology that feeds his self-esteem. That he abandons the scriptures by doing this is of no account to him. That he prefers his glory to that of God is precisely his problem. That attitude is part of man's corrupt nature, and he will cling to it until his dying breath, unless (for this is also of sovereign grace) God grinds his pride to pieces under the hammer blows of his irresistible grace.

Just as the truth of sovereign grace was victorious at Dordt and Westminster but soon fell before the onrush of Arminianism, so the doctrine of the well-meant offer has been victorious in much of the church world.

Chapter 14

Analysis and Positive Statement

A great deal of confusion is present today in the ecclesiastical world concerning the well-meant offer. Some insist that any denial of the well-meant offer is hyper-Calvinism. This has become so common that people who hear of anyone's denying the well-meant offer instinctively and with a knee-jerk reaction brand him as a hyper-Calvinist.

True hyper-Calvinists believe that it is proper and right to limit the preaching to only the elect. Such are the Gospel Standard people in England and the United States.[1] However, a denial of the well-meant offer does not automatically place one in the camp of the hyper-Calvinist. Many who deny that the preaching of the gospel is a well-meant offer emphatically assert that the gospel is to be preached and must be preached to all to whom God in his good pleasure sends it. This truth is

---

1   For a discussion of this subject, see David J. Engelsma, *Hyper-Calvinism and the Call of the Gospel*, 14–24.

incorporated into the Canons of Dordt, to which confession the Protestant Reformed Churches wholeheartedly subscribe.

> Moreover, the promise of the gospel is, that whosoever believeth in Christ crucified shall not perish, but have everlasting life. This promise, together with the command to repent and believe, ought to be declared and published to all nations, and to all persons promiscuously and without distinction, to whom God out of his good pleasure sends the gospel.[2]

> It is not the fault of the gospel, nor of Christ offered therein, nor of God, who calls men by the gospel, and confers upon them various gifts, that those who are called by the ministry of the Word refuse to come and be converted. The fault lies in themselves; some of whom when called, regardless of their danger, reject the Word of life; others, though they receive it, suffer it not to make a lasting impression on their heart; therefore, their joy, arising only from a temporary faith, soon vanishes, and they fall away; while others choke the seed of the Word by perplexing cares and the pleasures of this world, and produce no fruit. This our Saviour teaches in the parable of the sower (Matt. 13).[3]

This truth is also clearly taught in scripture. There is a powerful passage in Ezekiel 3:17–19 that places the blood of those who go lost on the head of the preacher who does not warn the wicked of his evil way. Only by warning the wicked can a preacher escape the responsibility for the destruction of the wicked man.

---

2   Canons of Dordt 2.5, in Schaff, *Creeds of Christendom*, 3:586.

3   Canons of Dordt 3–4.9, in ibid., 3:589.

17. Son of man, I have made thee a watchman unto the house of Israel: therefore hear the word at my mouth, and give them warning from me.

18. When I say unto the wicked, Thou shalt surely die; and thou givest him not warning, nor speakest to warn the wicked from his wicked way, to save his life; the same wicked man shall die in his iniquity; but his blood will I require at thine hand.

19. Yet if thou warn the wicked, and he turn not from his wickedness, nor from his wicked way, he shall die in his iniquity; but thou hast delivered thy soul.

How much clearer could the Lord make it when he gave his church her marching orders: "Go...into all the world, and preach the gospel to every creature" (Mark 16:15)?

The Protestant Reformed Churches have always insisted that the gospel must be preached to everyone to whom God is pleased to send it. I fear that the charge of hyper-Calvinism is hurled at those who reject the free offer because it is easier to label someone with a derogatory name than to enter into the teachings of the confessions and carefully exegete the scriptures and examine the arguments against a well-meant offer in order to answer them. So many times people pin the name onto those who deny the well-meant offer, and that is considered sufficient to ban the position from serious theological consideration. It is the easy way out of their obligation to prove from scripture and the confessions that they are right. But they are unable to do this.

Several things must be noticed about the general proclamation of the gospel.

First, according to Canons 2.5, the gospel is the general proclamation of a particular promise: the promise is only to those who believe and repent, that is, the elect in whom God works faith and repentance. While the gospel is publicly proclaimed, it is the public proclamation of a particular promise that God makes only to his people and that is theirs in the way of faith and repentance.

Second, "offered" in Canons 3–4.9 means "presented" or "proclaimed," which is the meaning of the Latin word *offere*. Christ is publicly presented in the gospel and proclaimed as the one in whom God works the great work of salvation. Such a proclamation and presentation of Christ in the gospel is not a Christ for all, but a Christ in whom God works salvation for those who believe in him and repent of their sins. Thus he is publicly presented as the one in whom God works salvation for believers.

Third, this is entirely in keeping with the character and nature of the gospel. The gospel is the power of God unto salvation to all who believe (Rom. 1:16). The gospel is not a lecture on a theological subject or a learned dissertation on a given text. It is emphatically preaching, and preaching is the means God is pleased to use to call his people out of darkness into salvation in Christ. Preaching is God's sovereign and efficacious means to bring salvation and heavenly glory to those who belong to Christ.

To make the preaching an offer robs the gospel of this great power and reduces it to an insipid expression of God's desire to save all those who hear. When the gospel is reduced to an expression of God's saving love for all, this makes the sovereign God of the gospel a pleading, begging, and seeking God who earnestly entreats the sinner to turn from his way and accept the offered salvation. God wants to save all, and the gospel expresses his intention and earnest longing to save everyone who hears. However, God can do very little except stand helplessly by and wait for man to accept or reject the offered salvation. If man accepts, salvation is granted him. But he may very well reject it. Thus his reaction to the gospel stands outside God's power and sovereign determination.

This conception of the gospel is thoroughly Arminian because it denies the truth of irresistible grace. It is Arminian because it ascribes to man the power to accept the gospel. Thus it denies man's utter depravity and inability to do any good. It is Arminian because it makes salvation dependent on the free will of man.

Ultimately these matters concern who God is. Is the sovereign God of heaven and earth, the maker and sustainer of all, the God who gives life and breath and upholds us every step of our earthly sojourn, a helpless God who cannot save? Such a view of God is an idol, the creation of men's proud imaginations. Such a view destroys the God of the scriptures and reduces him to a pleading beggar. This is a terrible sin that brings down the wrath of God on those who make him such a weak being that he is as putty in the hands of man.

Those who want to maintain the well-meant offer of the gospel and still go under the name of Calvinist or Reformed try to get around this terrible evil by saying that the faith and repentance necessary to receive Christ are gifts that God works in the hearts of his people. They say that the gospel offers Christ to everyone, and the gospel forcefully expresses that God's desire and intention are to bring everyone to salvation. But God works the necessary faith to receive the gospel only in the hearts of the elect, so that only they receive the offered salvation and are saved.

But this evasion will never do. This conception is a strange idea of God. God wants desperately to save a man, and he expresses his desire and deep longing to him. God earnestly and longingly does everything he can to make that man accept Christ as his savior. But God does not give that man the necessary faith for salvation. What kind of god is this? Can anyone imagine a god who so deeply and passionately wants to save a man but withholds from him the one thing necessary to be saved? It is within God's power to give faith, but he refrains from doing so. What kind of a husband would I be if I earnestly longed for the health of my wife who is dying from cancer, when I had in my power to restore her to health but refused? I would be branded by all men as a monster and probably would be brought before the judge and indicted on a charge of negligent homicide. Yet thus men present God.

Still more, the gospel is the promise of salvation in Christ. Does God promise faith and repentance as part of salvation? Are faith and repentance part of salvation and therefore part of the promise? If they are, then through the gospel as the power of God unto salvation, all of salvation is freely given, including faith and repentance. But when one makes the promise of the gospel dependent on the conditions of faith and repentance, he separates faith and repentance from salvation and makes them prerequisites to salvation. If faith and repentance are not part of salvation, they are the works of man. Faith and repentance are either part of the promise, sovereignly worked and given irresistibly through the gospel, or they are conditions to the promise and thus the works of man.

The well-meant offer is necessarily conditional, because although God desires the salvation of all who hear the gospel and makes salvation available for all who hear, not everyone is saved. Many reject the gospel in spite of the most sincere overtures and expressions of God's love for them. Because grace always accompanies the gospel offer, many reject the gospel even though they are the objects of God's grace. Thus the offer is conditional, dependent on faith and repentance, and thus faith and repentance are the works of man. The well-meant offer is inherently Arminian and a denial of all that has ever been true of the sovereignty of grace as set forth by Calvinism.

It is no wonder that those who have consistently held to a well-meant offer have inevitably drifted into the Arminian camp. Wherever the well-meant offer has been maintained, Arminianism has raised its ugly head. This was true of the Arminians condemned by the Synod of Dordt, for they were the ones who maintained conditional salvation.[4] This was true of the Amyraldians, whose influence extended to England, Europe, and the Netherlands. This is true in the history of the Reformed churches in the United States. That such a conditional salvation has led to Arminianism in the Christian Reformed Church is evident, for example, from the failure of the denomination to condemn a form of universal atonement as it appeared in the 1960s. We can come to only one conclusion: the necessary conditionality of the well-meant offer is essentially Arminian and a denial of Calvinism.

As Augustine insisted, what God wills to do, he does. Nothing can prevent God from executing his will.

The error of a well-meant offer always results in maintaining universal atonement and denying limited, or particular, atonement, because salvation intended for all must also be salvation purchased for all. If God through the gospel offers salvation to everyone who hears, along with the intent and expressed desire to save all, salvation must be available. If it is not, the whole offer is a farce, for God offers what he does not have, which makes

---

4   The word *condition* never appears in the Canons of Dordt except in the mouths of the Arminians (Canons 1, error 4, and Canons 2, error 3, in *Confessions and Church Order*, 160, 165).

God a liar and the offer a fake. Thus the cross of Christ and the redemption he accomplished become universal in extent.

If the cross of Jesus Christ is for all and yet all are not saved, the cross is robbed of its power. Jesus took upon himself the sins of his people and suffered in their place the wrath of God that should have come upon them. By his death he paid in full for all their sins, and he earned for them everlasting blessedness in the kingdom he established by his blood.

All those who hold to the well-meant offer deny the efficacy of Christ's sacrifice. He bore the sins of the whole world. He endured the wrath of God that the whole world deserves. He paid in full for every man. He earned eternal life in heaven for everyone. Yet some people go to hell. That can only mean that the work of Christ is totally ineffective, for many never receive what Christ earned.

The conclusion can only be that Christ did not take upon himself the sins of every person; that he did not bear God's wrath at all; that he earned nothing; that his death was a waste and useless for the majority of people. Then Calvary is lost and of no account and of no value.

Those who face this dilemma argue that while the cross is for everyone in sufficiency and intention, it is effective only for the elect. But what kind of nonsense is that? I have sufficient money to feed ten thousand people for a year. I intend also to do that, so that ten thousand people will not live on the brink of starvation. But when the time comes to spend the money and feed the poor, I spend only enough to feed one hundred and let the rest starve. How foolish.

Of special concern is the truth of unconditional election, or predestination. While it is true that the U of TULIP speaks only of unconditional election, reprobation has always been a part of the truth of predestination. The Canons define both as two parts of the same decree. The well-meant offer denies both. It denies reprobation because if God's sovereign purpose is not to save some, including some who hear the gospel, God's purpose in offering them salvation is meaningless and insincere. On the one hand, God determines not to save; on the other hand, God determines to save. On the one hand, God's will is not to save; on the other hand, God's will is to save. The result is that where the well-meant offer is taught reprobation is denied.

This is what has happened in the Christian Reformed Church. The truth of reprobation is hardly ever preached now, if at all. Seminary professor Harry Boer made a specific attack against this doctrine in 1977 when he asked the synod to strike the doctrine of reprobation from the Canons.[5] While synod refused to do that, it put its stamp of approval on a report of a study committee, which contained a definition of reprobation completely out of keeping with the historic definition of the doctrine and with the truth as it is taught in the Canons.[6] Synod in effect approved conditional reprobation, the very view that the Arminians had maintained and that our fathers at Dordt had repudiated.

If reprobation is denied, election falls by the way. They are two parts of one truth. The Canons of Dordt take the position that the one decree includes both election and reprobation.

> That some receive the gift of faith from God, and others do not receive it, proceeds from God's eternal decree [notice the singular *decree*, not the plural *decrees*]...

---

5   For Boer's gravamen to the synod of the Christian Reformed Church against the doctrine of reprobation as taught in the Canons of Dordt, see *Acts of Synod 1977* (Grand Rapids, MI: Board of Publications of the Christian Reformed Church), 665–79.

6   *Acts of Synod 1980* (Grand Rapids MI: Board of Publications of the Christian Reformed Church), 73–76.

According to which decree he graciously softens the hearts of the elect, however obstinate, and inclines them to believe, while he leaves the non-elect in his just judgment to their own wickedness and obduracy.[7]

The well-meant offer cannot bear the truth of election for the same reason it militates against reprobation. On the one hand, God purposes to save only his people chosen in Christ; on the other hand, he purposes to save all men. One will is to save some; another will is to save all men. Because the two are contradictory, both cannot be maintained. Thus the truth of sovereign election is sacrificed on the altar of the well-meant offer.

Those who hold to the well-meant offer and still want to retain some semblance of being Calvinistic and Reformed make a distinction between the will of God's decree and the will of his command, or as is sometimes said, between God's decretive will and his preceptive will. According to this idea, God's decretive will purposes the salvation of only the elect, while God's preceptive will purposes the salvation of all who hear the gospel. Thus God has two wills that are in direct conflict.

This problem is supposedly solved by an apparent contradiction. But this sort of argumentation ultimately leads to theological skepticism.[8] If there is contradiction possible at such a critical juncture of the truth, there are contradictions possible at any juncture of the truth. Then man can be both totally depraved and relatively good. Then grace is both resistible and irresistible. Then God is both triune and not triune. Then justification is by faith alone and also by faith and works. Then the atonement of Christ is both efficacious and ineffectual. But this

---

7   Canons of Dordt 1.6, in Schaff, *Creeds of Christendom*, 3:582.
8   For further discussion of this point, see Hanko, *For Thy Truth's Sake*, 199–229.

makes any knowledge of the truth impossible and mires one in the slime of subjectivism and skepticism. This does not mean that the distinction itself in God's will is invalid. Scripture indicates that within the one will of God, we may distinguish between God's will of decree and God's will of precept. The danger of evil enters when one sets these two over against each other so that they indicate two separate wills of God that conflict with each other. But the distinction must be maintained because it has importance for the present subject.[9] This error of two wills in God is not a new and recent heresy, but it goes back to the old heresy of Amyraldism, which has had devastating consequences on the history of doctrine in Reformed and Presbyterian churches.

Those who deny the well-meant offer of the gospel nevertheless maintain that the gospel is preached and must be preached to all creatures to whom God in his good pleasure is pleased to send it. That is, the gospel is and must be preached to many more than those whom it is God's purpose to save.

Throughout the history of the world, the gospel has by no means been brought to every person. This is also a problem the advocates of a well-meant offer cannot satisfactorily answer. If God expresses his desire to save all men, and if his desire is serious, well-meant, and truly an expression of his love and grace, it seems appropriate to the nature of God that he would express

---

9   For a detailed examination of God's will of decree and his will of precept, see Homer C. Hoeksema, "The Simplicity of God's Will and the 'Free Offer,'" *Protestant Reformed Theological Journal* 9, no. 2 (April 1976): 18–36; 10, no. 1 (November 1976): 1–16; 10, no. 2 (April 1977): 25–47; 11, no. 1 (November 1977): 16–26; 12, no. 2 (April 1979): 28–34; 13, no. 2 (April 1980): 38–48; 15, no. 1 (November 1981): 34–44; 16, no. 1 (November 1982): 13–17; 16, no. 2 (April 1983): 27–43; 17, no. 1 (November 1983): 19–32; 17, no. 2 (April 1984): 4–16; 18, no. 1 (November 1984): 14–22; 18, no. 2 (April 1985): 3–13; 19, no. 1 (November 1985): 3–15.

his desire to all men and not only to those to whom the gospel comes. Yet the gospel does not come to everyone.

That was true in the old dispensation, during which only relatively few heard the gospel. Far and away the majority of people who lived then never received the gospel, for the gospel was bound up in the types and shadows of Israel's ceremonial life and was therefore limited to the nation of Israel. The gospel came only to Israelites.

The same is true in the new dispensation. Although from the very beginning of its history the church has obeyed the command of Christ to go into the entire world and preach the gospel, that could not be accomplished immediately. In fact, even today there are remote tribes that still have not heard the gospel preached. This is because God in his good pleasure determines where his gospel is to be preached (Canons 2.5). He does that today just as certainly as he did when the Holy Spirit forbade the gospel to be preached in Asia on Paul's second missionary journey (Acts 16:6).

Why is it important for the gospel to be preached to more people than the elect? Some have answered that it is an inevitable fall-out from the preaching. It is impossible for the gospel to be preached to only elect, because the gospel is preached to mixed audiences, and the preachers do not know who in these audiences are elect and reprobate. Therefore, while it is unimportant and unnecessary that the gospel comes to more than the elect, there is little or nothing one can do about it. Besides, the reprobate cannot believe the gospel.

This is a terribly wrong and evil caricature of preaching. Never must we take this position, for it implies that God cannot do anything about the promiscuous preaching of the gospel to elect and reprobate alike, although he would prefer a different way. It is also a denial of the Canons of Dordt, which state that "the promise of the gospel…ought to be declared and published to all nations, and to all persons promiscuously and without distinction, to whom God out of his good pleasure sends the gospel."[10] It is a divine must. It is God's will.

We may not go to the opposite extreme and say that God's justice requires all men to have a chance to be saved. The idea is that God cannot justly send anyone to hell unless that person has heard the gospel and has rejected it or accepted it. God is just only if each person has a chance to accept Christ. This idea fits in perfectly with the well-meant offer. Yet it is so commonly heard today that it seems almost ingrained in people's thinking.

But this simply is untrue. On the one hand, the scriptures plainly teach that all men are guilty in Adam, apart from any guilt they may accumulate because of their sins, and this guilt in Adam is sufficient to send every man to hell. This is taught clearly in Romans 5:12–14:

12. Wherefore, as by one man sin entered into the world, and death by sin; and so death passed upon all men, for that all have sinned:
13. (For until the law sin was in the world: but sin is not imputed when there is no law.
14. Nevertheless death reigned from Adam to Moses, even over them that had not sinned after the similitude of Adam's transgression, who is the figure of him that was to come.

On the other hand, apart from that guilt, the wicked who never hear the gospel are confronted daily with the obligation to love and to serve God. This knowledge of God that all men possess is made known by the creation, which clearly testifies of

---

10 Canons of Dordt 2.5, in Schaff, *Creeds of Christendom*, 3:586.

God's eternal power and Godhead (Rom. 1:18–25). It is true that no man can be saved apart from the gospel, but this does not alter the fact that through the creation all men know that God alone is God and that he alone must be served. That they cannot serve God is not due to anything but their total depravity, for which they are responsible in Adam.

Romans 1 gives the reason for God's making himself known to all men through creation. The reason is not to give every man a chance to be saved or to prepare man for the gospel. Verse 20 says that God's reason is that all men will be without excuse in the judgment day. All men know their calling to worship God, but they refuse and change God's glory into idols.

It is God's will that many more than the elect hear the gospel proclaimed. God is pleased to have all who hear the gospel confronted with Christ and with the specific command to repent from their sins and believe in Christ. Not only the elect, but also the reprobate who hear the gospel, must be specifically and concretely commanded to turn from their evil ways and to believe in Christ. They cannot do this apart from God's work of regeneration and conversion, but they nevertheless must obey God.

Throughout this book I have always insisted that the original meaning of the word *offer* is entirely biblical. Christ is *presented* in the gospel to all who hear. He is presented and proclaimed to elect and reprobate. God wills this because through the presentation of Christ as the only one in whom there is salvation, all men who hear the gospel are placed before the solemn obligation to repent and believe. This is why Peter, in his great sermon on Pentecost, preached repentance and faith to all who heard him that day (Acts 2:38). All who hear the gospel stand before the question, what will you do with Christ?

The question remains: why is it God's purpose to confront all those who hear the gospel with the command to repent and believe? Why must those whom God has purposed not to save, as well as those whom God does save, be commanded to repent and believe?

The answer is not that these select people are given an opportunity to be saved, or that for some unspecified purpose God gives them a chance that is not given to those who never hear the gospel. This interpretation introduces into the preaching of the gospel an Arminian element that is completely antipathetic to the teaching of God's word. God does not give people a chance to be saved when he knows they cannot and will not believe.

The answer is that God always maintains the demands of his law. God originally created man upright and capable of doing all things God required of him. Man by Satan's temptation of Adam fell into sin. Although man fell and by his fall brought upon himself total depravity, so that he cannot keep the law in any respect, God does not and cannot change his demands. This would be out of keeping with the holiness of God.

Suppose that I contract with a carpenter to build a house for me at a cost of $150,000. The carpenter informs me that he cannot proceed with building until I advance him the total cost of $150,000 so he can begin building the house. Instead of using the money for building, he takes a round-the-world trip and spends all the money given to him. Upon his return, I have the right to insist that he build my house. He may object and plead that he is unable because he no longer possesses the necessary money. But this does not alter my demand in the least. I will tell him, "I gave you all that was necessary to build my house. You squandered the money on your own pleasures. That is not my fault; it is yours. Now build my house."

This is no less true of God. God gave all men in Adam everything necessary to serve God. That man is incapable of serving him is not God's fault, but man's. According to God's holiness and justice, he must insist that man serve him. Because of sin, God's demand to serve him involves the command to repent of sin and believe on Jesus Christ. For God to require anything less than this would be a denial of his justice and holiness.

It is characteristic of Arminians always to identify obligation with ability. They say that God may obligate man to do only what he is able to do. But this is very far from the truth. The Heidelberg Catechism states the matter succinctly:

Q. Doth not God, then, wrong man by requiring of him in his law that which he can not perform?
A. No; for God so made man that he could perform it; but man, through the instigation of the devil, by willful disobedience deprived himself and all his posterity of this power.[11]

The command to repent of sin and believe in Christ is rooted in God's original command to Adam and to all men to obey him. This command God continues to maintain. Obedience to God is man's calling and responsibility, for he is a creature dependent upon God who created him. Because he remains a creature, dependent on God, he cannot escape the demand to obey God in everything.

Through the command that comes to all who hear the gospel, God accomplishes his purpose. We must look at this from two sides. On man's side, his refusal to obey the command of the gospel places him unmistakably where he is justly sentenced to everlasting condemnation in hell—not as if he does not deserve hell already because of his sin in Adam and because of his refusal to obey the testimony of God in the things that belong to the

11 Heidelberg Catechism Q&A 9, in ibid., 3:310.

creation. But the command comes much more clearly through the gospel, because in the gospel God presents Christ crucified to accomplish salvation.

To repent of sin and believe in Christ is the way of salvation. When man refuses to do this, he shows his deep sin and bitter enmity. He demonstrates unmistakably that he hates God and his Christ, that he will have no part of God's salvation, that he despises everything of God and his truth, and that he prefers an eternity in hell to repenting of his evil way, which he loves. When therefore he is cast into hell for his terrible sin, no one can say that this is unjust. He receives what he wants and what he has justly coming to him.

If it is objected once again that he is incapable of believing in Christ and turning from his evil way, then the answer is, once again, who is to blame? Is not the sinner to blame? His sin and depravity are not God's fault but his own.

Or the question may be asked, what difference does it make if the gospel comes to such a man when he already shows his hatred by refusing to worship God after knowing him through the created things? Why does God want him also to hear the gospel? The answer is that sin must appear completely as sin. It must be evident that sin is the terrible power that it is. The sinner rejects God even when God provides a way of escape, and man's judgment as a result is greater. Jesus says in Matthew 11:21–24 that it will be more tolerable for the heathen in the jungles of Africa than for the citizens of America and Europe.

Perhaps it is objected that the command to repent and serve God is not clear enough in creation to understand precisely what God means. But in the preaching of the gospel, the command to repent and believe in Christ is so clearly set forth that no mistake can be made. When the ungodly reject the demand to repent and believe in Christ, it becomes unmistakably clear that man is so wicked that he will disobey God's command no matter how clearly it comes to him.

Sin is so terrible that when Christ, God's Son, was sent for salvation, wicked men took him in their filthy hands and nailed him to a cross. When that cross is preached as God's way of salvation, man will trample underfoot the blood of the covenant and crucify the Son of God afresh (Heb. 6:4–6).

God does everything necessary, apart from man's sin, to make salvation clear and unmistakable. When Isaiah writes about what God has done with his vineyard, he concludes with the words of God:

3. And now, O inhabitants of Jerusalem, and men of Judah, judge, I pray you, betwixt me and my vineyard.
4. What could have been done more to my vineyard, that I have not done in it? wherefore, when I looked that it should bring forth grapes, brought it forth wild grapes?
5. And now go to; I will tell you what I will do to my vineyard: I will take away the hedge thereof, and it shall be eaten up; and break down the wall thereof, and it shall be trodden down:
6. And I will lay it waste: it shall not be pruned, nor digged; but there shall come up briers and thorns: I will also command the clouds that they rain no rain upon it. (Isa. 5:3–6)

We must also consider God's viewpoint. God always accomplishes his sovereign purpose. Nothing is outside his will and nothing takes place without his sovereign determination. With respect to this subject, this means that the decree of reprobation must be accomplished. By means of the command of the gospel that comes to all who hear, God accomplishes his purpose in reprobation. God has determined from all eternity to save a people. But God has also determined from all eternity to damn the wicked to eternal hell in the way of their sins.

This requires explanation. Reprobation cannot be separated from the sins of the wicked. Yet we must be careful to understand this. The sins of the wicked are not the cause or condition of reprobation, so that God reprobates on account of sin and unbelief. This is the position of the Arminians that is emphatically refuted by the fathers of Dordt in the Canons. The scriptures abhor conditional reprobation because it detracts from the absolute sovereignty of God.

Nor may it be asserted that the decree of reprobation is the cause of the sin of the wicked. This makes God the author of sin, something that the Canons brand as blasphemy. Rather, we must insist that reprobation is decreed and sovereignly accomplished in the way of man's sin, so that while God is sovereign in his decree, man goes to hell because he and he alone has sinned and must bear the responsibility for sin.

This difficult question involves the relationship between God's sovereign counsel and man's sin, for which man alone is responsible. There is a mystery here that our feeble minds cannot begin to fathom. We must not at this point fall back into the error of apparent contradiction. God's absolute sovereignty and man's accountability are not contradictory, although the relationship between the two is beyond our comprehension. But scripture is clear enough on the point that also sin lies within the scope of God's decree and purpose. Yet God so decrees and works that man remains forever responsible (Acts 2:23; 4:27–28).

What needs to be emphasized is that through the preaching of the gospel, with the command to repent and believe, God accomplishes his sovereign purpose. The gospel is intended by God not only to save his elect, but also to harden the reprobate. It is exactly this command of the gospel that comes to all that serves as God's means to harden in sin. Because the gospel presents Christ as the way of salvation, and because all men everywhere are commanded to believe in Christ, the gospel works as God's power to damn the wicked in the way of their sin and impenitence.

Paul speaks of this in 2 Corinthians 2:14–17:

14. Now thanks be unto God, which always causeth us to triumph in Christ, and maketh manifest the savour of his knowledge by us in every place.
15. For we are unto God a sweet savour of Christ, in them that are saved, and in them that perish:
16. To the one we are the savour of death unto death; and to the other the savour of life unto life. And who is sufficient for these things?
17. For we are not as many, which corrupt the word of God: but as of sincerity, but as of God, in the sight of God speak we in Christ.

This is why Peter wrote that Christ preached is "a stone of stumbling, and a rock of offence, even to them which stumble at the word, being disobedient: whereunto also they were appointed" (1 Pet. 2:8). And this is why John wrote in John 12:37–41:

37. But though he had done so many miracles before them, yet they believed not on him:
38. That the saying of Esaias the prophet might be fulfilled, which he spake, Lord, who hath believed our report? and to whom hath the arm of the Lord been revealed?

39. Therefore they could not believe, because that Esaias said again,
40. He hath blinded their eyes, and hardened their heart; that they should not see with their eyes, nor understand with their heart, and be converted, and I should heal them.
41. These things said Esaias, when he saw his glory, and spake of him.

Therefore, when the gospel is preached promiscuously, and all who hear are placed before the command to repent and believe, God accomplishes his sovereign purpose in those who refuse to believe and in their disobedience. This is why the gospel must be preached to many more than the elect.

This command of God that comes to all who hear the gospel is serious. God is not playing games with men when he commands them to repent and believe. God is not merely toying with their emotions and eternal estate. God means exactly what he says. He is so serious about it that refusal ends in eternal death. The Canons emphasize this:

> As many as are called by the gospel are unfeignedly called; for God hath most earnestly and truly shown in his Word what will be acceptable to him, namely, that all who are called should comply with the invitation. He, moreover, seriously promises eternal life and rest to as many as shall come to him, and believe on him.[12]

This brings up another question that has troubled some. Is not God's serious and unfeigned call to repent of sin and turn

---

12 Canons of Dordt 3–4.8, in ibid., 3:589.

to Christ an expression of God's will and desire to save all men? How is this different from the well-meant offer?

The difference is great and crucial. Earlier I mentioned that it is not wrong to make a distinction between God's decretive will and God's preceptive will, God's will of decree and God's will of command, as long as these two aspects of God's will are not placed in contradiction with each other so that they become two separate wills.

Bearing this in mind, it is certainly correct and according to scripture to say that God's will of command is that all men obey him, keep his commandments, walk in his way, and love him with all their hearts and minds and souls and strength. If they sin, as they always do, this will of God's command surely means that men must turn from their evil ways, repent of their sins, and seek their salvation only in Christ.

This command of God is his morally perfect will for men. Because God is supremely holy and without sin, because he loves only what is right and good and according to his law, he delights only in the good and hates all evil. When he insists that all men serve him alone as God, repent of their sins, and seek their salvation only in Jesus Christ, this is his good and morally holy will. He can do nothing else, for he is the Holy One of Israel. It would sully and stain his holiness for God to say, "It is quite all right with me if you continue in your sins. In fact, it is understandable that you walk in sin, live in rebellion against me, and trample underfoot my righteous ways." No man would ever say that this is God's will. His will is as he is: holy, just, good, righteous, and perfectly right.

This command, which comes to all men, to repent of sin and turn to Christ is the expression of God's holy and just will for the sinner. There is fundamentally (and I speak in all reverence) nothing else that God can do but to demand holiness of men. It is his morally holy will that men do what is right.

This is in perfect harmony with the will of his decree, because it is exactly through this morally holy will of his command that God sovereignly executes his eternal will of reprobation. If his will were anything less than morally holy, the decree of reprobation could not be executed through it.

Through the will of his command God accomplishes the will of his decree. He gives to the elect the spiritual power to repent and believe, and he hardens the reprobate in the way of their unbelief. But this is not the well-meant offer that teaches that God desires and intends the salvation of all who hear the gospel, that because of his love and grace for them he offers them Christ as their salvation, and that it is his purpose and will to save them. This is Arminian in every respect and a resurrection of the old heresy of Amyraldism, which destroys all the truth of the gospel.

One more point closely connected to the well-meant offer must be addressed. The well-meant offer gives a decidedly wrong idea of scripture. Scripture as a whole and the following texts in particular are often presented as an offer of the gospel addressed to all men.

1. Ho, every one that thirsteth, come ye to the waters, and he that hath no money; come ye, buy, and eat; yea, come, buy wine and milk without money and without price.

2. Wherefore do ye spend money for that which is not bread? and your labour for that which satisfieth not? hearken diligently unto me, and eat ye that which is good, and let your soul delight itself in fatness.

3. Incline your ear, and come unto me: hear, and your soul shall live; and I will make an everlasting

covenant with you, even the sure mercies of David. (Isa. 55:1–3)

"Come unto me, all ye that labour and are heavy laden, and I will give you rest" (Matt. 11:28). "And the Spirit and the bride say, Come. And let him that heareth say, Come. And let him that is athirst come. And whosoever will, let him take the water of life freely" (Rev. 22:17). Because the scriptures are preeminently the revelation of Christ, Christ in the whole of scripture is said to be offered to all.

However, the address of these texts, is very particular—limited to a select group of people. Isaiah 55:1–3 specifically addresses those who are thirsty and have no money. Matthew 11:28 specifically addresses those who labor and are heavy laden. Revelation 22:17 specifically addresses the man who hears, who is thirsty, and whosoever wills.

It is possible to interpret these texts to refer to everyone in the world, or at least to everyone who hears the gospel. But this interpretation can only be made from a totally Arminian viewpoint. If everyone thirsts, is without money, is laboring and heavy laden, and wills to come to Christ, then everyone is capable of seeking salvation by himself. He has the power within himself to seek Christ, thirst for him, and will to come to him. Then the totally depraved sinner, apart from Christ's work of salvation, is capable of doing good, of exercising free will, and of coming to Christ by his initiative. This Arminian conception puts all the responsibility of salvation upon man, ascribes to him powers that he does not have, and makes God dependent on the sinner's choice.

When the texts are specific in their addresses, they are such because they are meant to be Christ's word only to specific people. Because no man can of himself thirst for Christ, come to the water, be burdened by his sin and guilt, and will to come, these spiritual virtues are dependent on the work of the Holy Spirit. Only the Spirit can work these powers within a man. But the Holy Spirit works these powers only in God's elect, in those for whom Christ died and who are efficaciously called by the Spirit in their hearts. By virtue of the Spirit's work, these people thirst for Christ, are heavy laden under the load of their sins, and will to come.

We may well ask why Christ works this way, that is, first working in his people a longing for salvation and then calling them to himself. The answer is, first, that God always deals with his people as rational and moral creatures, not as stocks and blocks. God does not take his people along the pathway of this life to glory in the same way a child pulls a mechanical toy across the floor. God wants his people to know and experience their salvation. He wants them to be conscious partakers of his grace so they may praise and bless his name for the salvation he gives to them. They will hear these words with eagerness and joy.

Second, while God's people are in this world they are imperfect. Even though they are regenerated and converted, the work of salvation in them is only in principle. They are still in their flesh, and in their flesh dwells no good thing. There is much sin in them that strives for mastery in their lives, pulls them in the direction of this world, and often causes them to fall deeply into sin. Against the evil in their flesh they must constantly struggle; and when they fall into sin, they must repent of their sins and turn to Christ. Christ's call is balm to their broken hearts. Overwhelmed by the awareness of their sins and unworthiness, they tremble in fear and wonder whether Christ will receive them. They hardly dare come to him.

Third, only through repentance and sorrow for sin can God's people know their salvation in Christ. Without a deep consciousness of their sin and an overwhelming awareness of their unworthiness, they have no need of Christ, no consciousness of their utter dependence on him, and no sense of the truth that salvation is to be found only in him.

God deals with his people through the gospel, addressing them in this life, in their struggles and sins, in their needs and troubles, in the consciousness of their sins and helplessness. Through his call he brings them back to himself, restores them to grace and favor, shows them his great love and mercy, gives them his full and free salvation, and makes them conscious of it.

Thus the elect, in whom the Spirit works, thirst for God as a hart pants for water brooks. They are without money because they know their hopeless state, their utter inability to save themselves, and their total dependence on God. They are laboring and heavy laden because the burden of sin is intolerable, too heavy to bear, too great to carry as they walk the pathway of this life. They will to come because they have seen the total futility of life apart from God and the hopelessness of the wicked world that so often attracts them to its pleasures and lusts. But all these things are true of them because the Spirit of Christ has put these characteristics into their hearts and lives.

When the gospel is reduced to an offer, the work of the Holy Spirit is minimized, if not denied. The preaching of the gospel is always accompanied with the internal operation of the Holy Spirit. The Spirit sovereignly accomplishes God's purpose, whether in the hardening of the reprobate or in the saving of the elect. The word of God always accomplishes God's purpose. "So shall my word be that goeth forth out of my mouth: it shall not return unto me void, but it shall accomplish that which I please, and it shall prosper in the thing whereto I sent it" (Isa. 55:11). But when the gospel is only an expression of what God would like to do, what can the Holy Spirit do with that? He cannot harden, because that is not God's intention. He cannot save, because the gospel presents only what God would like to do, not what he actually does. All the Holy Spirit can do is give grace to every hearer, which leaves the responsibility to accept or reject the gospel to the hearer.

The scriptures are addressed to God's people, not to all men. The scriptures are the infallibly inspired record of the revelation of Jehovah God in the face of the Lord Jesus Christ as the God who saves his people from their sins. Because scripture is this, it is God's word of hope and promise to them. It is the only light that shines in this dark world of hopeless despair. It is God's great grace and mercy revealed in Christ to those whom he has chosen to be his own inheritance. It is the Bridegroom's love letter to his elect and chosen bride for whom he died and to whom he comes tenderly and compassionately to save them.

Christ addresses his bride in her sins, struggles, troubles, and afflictions. Sometimes he encourages her; sometimes he sharply reprimands her; sometimes he comforts tenderly and compassionately; sometimes he calls to her with all the sweetness of his loving voice. But always his purpose is to lead her to him and to bring her to the joy of the salvation he has prepared for her.

Thus he calls his people by their spiritual names. In John 10 Jesus speaks of this under the figure of a shepherd and his sheep. He says that the sheep hear his voice, that he calls his sheep by name (literally, name by name, v. 3), that he is the good shepherd who gives his life for the sheep, who knows his sheep, and who is known of those who are his sheep (vv. 11, 14). These are the spiritual names of the people of God who belong to Christ. Scripture calls them those who thirst, who labor and are heavy laden, who mourn, and who hunger and thirst after righteousness.

Christ uses these spiritual names to address his people in scripture and in the preaching of the word, because when the preaching is addressed to Christ's people under these names, the Spirit of Christ works in the hearts of his people so they recognize themselves as hungering and thirsting, as laboring and heavy laden. Recognizing themselves as such, they know that Christ calls them, and they hear his word. Rejoicing, they come to him who is the fountain of all their life and the source of all their strength. They hear the word of the gospel: "Come unto me, all ye that labor and are heavy laden; and I will give you rest." As Christ works in their hearts so that they see the heavy burdens of sin that weigh upon them and crush them, they hear Christ call to them and recognize it as the call of their Lord. Joyfully and full of hope they flee to Christ and receive the promised rest.

This is the character of scripture. It is not a book addressed to all men, or even to all who hear the gospel. It is a love letter addressed by Christ to his elect bride.

This does not mean that when scripture is preached to many others besides the elect, by it all men are not confronted with the obligation to repent of sin and come to Christ. They surely are, for though many are called, few are chosen (Matt. 22:14). All men stand solemnly before the command to obey God, walk in his ways, and keep his commandments. That command to repent and believe is the command that Christ uses through his Spirit to bring his people to repentance and faith in him. The power of that word of the gospel, the power of God unto salvation (Rom. 1:16), even when it comes in the form of a command, is the power by which repentance and faith are worked in the elect. When the command of the gospel goes forth to come to Christ, all who come under the preaching hear that command. This is not only the nature of the preaching, but it is also God's purpose.

That one command, heard by all who hear the preaching, has a twofold effect. As it places the reprobate before the obligations of God's word, it is the means to harden them in their unbelief. That same command is heard by the elect, in whom Christ has begun his work of salvation and grace, and they obey with hearts made willing by God's gracious operations within them. God works both the willing and the doing in them (Phil. 2:13).

To reduce the preaching to a well-meant offer, therefore, is to rob the preaching and the scriptures of their beauty and power, of their comfort and hope, since these scriptures are the only light we have in the world. How wonderful it is to have the voice of Christ our savior speak to us! How wonderful it is to hear his voice addressed to us, calling us name by name! How wonderful it is to hear of his great mercy and love, his grace and compassion, addressed to us personally!

Christ is full of pity toward us in our sins, tender and compassionate even when we stray from him, moved to tears at our waywardness and foolishness. His love shines through when he rebukes us, for it is for our good. His patience with us knows no end, for we are all like sheep that have gone astray. He lifts us up and carries us back to the fold, though we deserve nothing of such great grace. His encouragement to us in all the difficulties of life comes as cooling streams in the parched wasteland of this world. His promise that he will be with us always and take us finally into his Father's house of many mansions lightens our darkest moments. His assurance that no man can pluck us out of his hand gives us courage and puts steel in our spines when we face the hordes of our enemies, who are so much stronger than we are. Who, understanding this, would want to reduce scripture to a mere offer? It is incredible that anyone, having tasted the good things of the gospel, can deal so disparagingly with the most blessed of all books.

Scripture is so full of passages that flatly and explicitly contradict the well-meant offer that it would be extremely strange, to say the least, if other passages taught it. God's scriptures are a unity, a harmonious whole, and a single revelation of God in Christ. If scripture contradicts itself and teaches opposing ideas, we could not have any confidence in scripture at all, and we would be reduced to theological agnosticism.

This study would be incomplete without looking at several texts that are often quoted in support of the well-meant offer.

The first is Ezekiel 33:11: "Say unto them, As I live, saith the Lord GOD, I have no pleasure in the death of the wicked; but that the wicked turn from his way and live: turn ye, turn ye from your evil ways; for why will ye die, O house of Israel?" No matter how this passage is taken, there is no offer of salvation in it. God swears an oath as the living God that he has no pleasure in the death of the wicked. His pleasure is that the wicked turn from their evil ways. Even if God's reference to the wicked is interpreted to mean all men, there is still no offer. Rather, in all sincerity God places before all men the command to repent from sin and turn from their evil ways. God's moral will is such that he has no pleasure in sin and demands holiness from men.

However, this text is addressed to "the house of Israel" and not to all men without distinction. The words are an answer to something that deeply worried the children of Israel: "If our transgressions and our sins be upon us, and we pine away in them, how should we then live?" (Ezek. 33:10). The children of Israel had departed from the ways of God's covenant and had made themselves worthy of God's wrath and displeasure. They were in Babylon, and in the agony of their sins, they wondered whether they would be received in favor. They knew they rightly deserved to die, and they were troubled by how they could be restored to life. They knew how undeserving they were. What child of God, after falling deeply into sin and coming again to the consciousness of how terrible his sin is before God, does not ask the same question? He wonders in the agony of his soul, "Is there any way out of my sin to life? Can God receive me again? If there is a way out, what is the way?"

In addressing those concerns, God said to Israel, "I have no pleasure in your death, but that you turn from your evil ways and live." God's gracious promise to those who turn from their evil ways and repent of their sins is precisely that they will be restored to life.

The second text used to promote a well-meant offer is Matthew 23:37 (and the parallel passage in Luke 13:34): "O Jerusalem, Jerusalem, thou that killest the prophets, and stonest them which are sent unto thee, how often would I have gathered thy children together, even as a hen gathereth her chickens under her wings, and ye would not!" It is difficult to understand exactly why the proponents of the well-meant offer quote this text. Presumably their argument goes something like this. Jesus wanted to gather to himself all the people of Jerusalem, and he expressed that divine desire and intention to save them. But he was prevented from doing that by their stubborn rebellion and unbelief. The conclusion is that if Jesus wanted to save all the inhabitants of Jerusalem, he surely offered salvation to all of them.

If this is the argument, it is immediately apparent that the offer is assumed. The text says nothing about an offer. Apart from this assumption, is it true that Jesus expressed his divine intention and purpose to save all the inhabitants of Jerusalem? The answer must be an emphatic no. The language of the text refutes this notion. Jesus did not say, "How often would I have gathered thee together." Instead he says, "How often would I have gathered *thy children* together." This is quite different.

By "Jerusalem" Jesus does not mean the inhabitants of

Jerusalem, but the city as the center of all Israel's political and ecclesiastical life. In more than one place in scripture, this city is pictured as a mother who brings forth children (see Gal. 4:24–27). In the old dispensation Jerusalem was the church of God. In Jesus' time it was the church that had become apostate and corrupt. It was the church from the viewpoint of her temple and sacrifices, priesthood and ceremonies, and feast days and cleansings, but as all those were polluted by the wicked scribes and Pharisees.

Jesus expressed his desire to save Jerusalem's children. The scribes and Pharisees fought bitterly against that at every step of his way. They fiercely resisted his efforts and finally nailed him to the cross. But does all this indicate that Jerusalem's children were never gathered by Jesus? Far from it. Jesus accomplished his purpose in spite of the wickedness of Jerusalem's leaders. We have only to read of the thousands of Jerusalem's children who were saved after Pentecost to understand that Jesus did what he had purposed to do. In Matthew 23:37 Jesus emphasized the terrible sin of Jerusalem, which was almost ripe for destruction and which would soon be razed to the ground. The people of Jerusalem not only rejected Christ, but they also did everything in their power to prevent their children from coming to Christ. Therefore, Jesus could tell them, "Behold, your house is left unto you desolate" (v. 38).

Defenders of the well-meant offer sometimes refer to Jesus' weeping over Jerusalem. Their argument seems to be that Jesus was sorry for Jerusalem's rejection of him and therefore wanted Jerusalem to repent. This is not the point of Jesus' sorrow, however. Jerusalem was a figure and type of the church, which is his body. It was the capital and center of the life of a nation that was uniquely favored of God (Rom. 9:4–5). That Jesus was filled with sorrow is not surprising. He was like us in all things except sin, and he felt the pain of being forsaken by his own country and people. "He came unto his own, and his own received him not"

(John 1:11). Some of this same pain is felt by those with roots in the Netherlands when they see that the land of their fathers—once the cradle of the Reformed faith—is apostate and morally bankrupt. It is an unwarranted conclusion that Jesus' sorrow implied his longing and desire to save the Jews.

The third text is 2 Peter 3:9: "The Lord is not slack concerning his promise, as some men count slackness; but is longsuffering to us-ward, not willing that any should perish, but that all should come to repentance." The argument of those who use this text to support a well-meant offer is that since God is unwilling to have anyone perish, he desires everyone to repent and to be saved. Therefore, he offers salvation to all men. But the text says nothing about an offer. Even if one interprets the words "any" and "all" as referring to all men, there is no mention whatsoever of an offer.

Is it true that "any" and "all" in this passage refer to all men? They most emphatically do not. In the context Peter says that scoffers will come in the last days and deny the second coming of Christ (2 Pet. 3:3–4). The basis for their argument is what modern evolutionists call the uniformitarian theory, that is, all things continue now as they were from the beginning of the creation. Peter shows that this is wrong and that all things do not continue as they were from the beginning of the creation, for the antediluvian world was "standing out of the water and in the water" and was destroyed by water, while "the heavens and the earth, which are now, by the same word are kept in store, reserved unto fire against the day of judgment" (vv. 5–7).

The members of the church of Peter's day were hard-pressed by persecution and were somewhat persuaded by those scoffers. The church was influenced by the scoffers because Jesus was expected to return any day, but he had not returned immediately. Thus the members thought the Lord was "slack concerning his promise." Peter assured them that this was not the case.

CORRUPTING THE WORD OF GOD

The people of God must remember that time as we know it does not govern the purpose and counsel of almighty God. One day is with the Lord as a thousand years and a thousand years as one day (2 Pet. 3:8). Even if the Lord should delay the coming of Christ for one thousand years, this would be but as a day with him. Emphatically the Lord is not slack concerning his promise, as some men count slackness. Besides, there is a good reason Christ does not come back immediately: there are many elect who must still be saved. If the Lord would come back too early, so to speak, there would be elect who would never be born and saved, for the return of Christ means the end of history, and thus also the end of marriage and the bringing forth of children. God does not want any of his elect to perish but wants them all to come to repentance. Christ will not return until that has happened.

It is clear, therefore, that "any" and "all" in 2 Peter 3:9 must refer to the elect, not to all men, and must be interpreted in the light of the word "us-ward." God is longsuffering to us, not willing that any of us should perish, but that all of us should come to repentance. This is so clearly the meaning of the text that only a superficial reading could interpret it another way.

This interpretation is further strengthened by what Peter wrote in verse 15: "Account that the longsuffering of our Lord is salvation." God's longsuffering is salvation. The apostle did not say that God's long-suffering desires salvation, wants salvation, or even intends to give salvation. But God's attribute of long-suffering is itself salvation.

If the promoters of the well-meant offer want to make God's long-suffering an attribute shown to all men, they will have to admit that because long-suffering is salvation, all those toward whom God is long-suffering are saved. Not even the most ardent defenders of the well-meant offer want to go as far as to say that

God's long-suffering toward the reprobate is their actual salvation. The only conclusion is that the long-suffering of God, which is salvation, is shown only "to us-ward." The result is that Christ does not return until all those for whom he died, given to him of the Father from all eternity, are born and brought to repentance. Then Christ will surely come to destroy this old world, create a new heavens and a new earth, and give to his saints the everlasting inheritance of that glorious creation.

There can be no doubt that both history and scripture stand opposed to the well-meant offer of the gospel. That the so-called offer is so generally received in our day can only be indicative of the sad state of affairs in the churches. Arminianism and Pelagianism have made devastating inroads. How sad it is that the truths of sovereign grace are no longer maintained and taught. How sad it is that God is robbed of his majesty and that man exalts himself to God's throne.

There is a terrible price to pay for this, for all Arminianism is incipient modernism. Those churches that have chosen the Arminian way have clearly demonstrated the truth of this, for already in them modernism is making its inroads. Modernism denies the Christ, tramples underfoot the blood of the covenant, and makes all that is holy an unholy thing. Upon such a church rests terrible judgments.

But the truth will triumph, and the gospel, which is the power of God unto salvation, will be God's means to save all who are ordained unto eternal life.

It is my hope and prayer that all who love the truth of scripture and the precious doctrines of sovereign grace may see the error of the well-meant offer of the gospel and reject it. May God bless these efforts to his glory and the cause of his precious gospel in the midst of the world.

About the Authors

—⟨⟩—

Herman Hanko was ordained into the ministry of the word and sacraments in 1955 and pastored Protestant Reformed churches in Grand Rapids, Michigan, and Doon, Iowa. For thirty-five years he taught New Testament and church history at the Theological School of the Protestant Reformed Churches. In retirement he continued to serve the church of Christ by preaching, lecturing, and writing.

Professor Hanko has authored the following publications of the Reformed Free Publishing Association:

Contending for the Faith: The Rise of Heresy and the Development of the Truth

Faith Made Perfect: Commentary on James

For Thy Truth's Sake: A Doctrinal History of the Protestant Reformed Churches

God's Everlasting Covenant of Grace

Justified unto Liberty: Commentary on Galatians

Mysteries of the Kingdom: An Exposition of Jesus' Parables

A Pilgrim's Manual: Commentary on 1 Peter

Portraits of Faithful Saints

Ready to Give an Answer: A Catechism of Reformed Distinctives (coauthor)

We and Our Children: The Reformed Doctrine of Infant Baptism

When You Pray: Scripture's Teaching on Prayer

———————

Mark Hoeksema was trained in the Theological School of the Protestant Reformed Churches and served pastorates in North Dakota and Iowa. He is the editor of the following publications of the Reformed Free Publishing Association: The *Unfolding Covenant History* series and the two-volume set on the book of Isaiah, *Redeemed with Judgment*. He has recently authored three Bible study guides on the books of Acts, Romans, and James and a commentary on the book of 2 Peter.

Select Annotated Bibliography

by Angus Stewart

Augustine. *The Enchiridion on Faith, Hope and Love.* Edited by Henry Paolucci. Translated by J. F. Shaw. Chicago, IL: Henry Regnery Co., 1961. Augustine of Hippo (354–430) in North Africa was undoubtedly the greatest theologian of the early church. Toward the end of his eventful life, he wrote a handbook for a Roman called Laurentius, summarizing the Christian faith around the three theological virtues (faith, hope, and love) and the Apostles' Creed. This work, which has been very popular in the church's history, contains a lengthy section (xciv–cvii) on eternal election and reprobation and God's omnipotence and immutability, which sharply opposes the free offer and its misinterpretation of 1 Timothy 2:4 and Matthew 23:37, in the light of scripture (especially Ps. 115:3; 135:6; Rom. 9).[1]

Calvin, John. *Calvin's Calvinism: God's Eternal Predestination and Secret Providence* together with *A Brief Reply* and *Reply to the Slanderous Reports.* Translated by Henry Cole. Second edition. Edited by Russell J. Dykstra. Jenison, MI: Reformed Free Publishing Association, 2009. This superb publication contains the French reformer's fullest and most detailed treatment of God's eternal predestination over against several Roman

---

1 For this excerpt, see "Augustine Versus a Desire of God to Save the Reprobate" (www.cprf.co.uk/articles/augustineenchiridion.htm).

Catholic theologians, who argue that God desires to convert everybody, appealing to the usual texts, especially 1 Timothy 2:4, on which Calvin (1509–64) faithfully follows the Augustinian exegesis. Part 1 of this book, *God's Eternal Predestination and Secret Providence* or the *Consensus Genevensis* (1552), its longest section, was sent forth with the consent of Geneva's Venerable Company of Pastors.[2]

Engelsma, David J. Hyper-Calvinism and the Call of the Gospel: An Examination of the Well-Meant Offer of the Gospel. Jenison, MI: Reformed Free Publishing Association, 2014. Though this book is mainly a theological and biblical refutation of the free offer, it does treat historical aspects of the issue, including, for example, the English hyper-Calvinists in the eighteenth century, Dutch Secession theologians in the nineteenth century, and developments in twentieth-century North American churches, especially the Christian Reformed Church and the Orthodox Presbyterian Church. It also contains chapters on the sound teaching on the gospel call by John Calvin, Francis Turretin, and Abraham Kuyper (1837–1920).

The Geneva Theses (1649). In *Reformed Confessions of the 16th and 17th Centuries in English Translation*, edited by James T. Dennison Jr., 4:413–22. Grand Rapids, MI: Reformation Heritage Books, 2014. This binding confession from Calvin's citadel explicitly and repeatedly rejects the free-offer view of God's will and love as taught by the Amyraldians and opposes their interpretation of Ezekiel 18:21, 33:11, 1 Timothy 2:4, and 2 Peter 3:9. The two pastors and theological professors who drafted the *Geneva Theses* were Antoine Léger (1594–1661) and Théodore

---

2 For quotations, see "The Free Offer: Calvin Vs. Pighius (and John Murray)" (www.cprf.co.uk/quotes/pighius.htm).

Tronchin (1582–1657), who was a Genevan delegate at the Synod of Dordt, which condemned Arminianism.[3]

Genke, Victor, and Francis X. Gumerlock, ed. and trans. *Gottschalk and a Medieval Predestination Controversy: Texts Translated From the Latin.* Milwaukee, WI: Marquette University Press, 2010. Saxon monk and missionary to Croatia and Bulgaria, Gottschalk of Orbais (c.808–c.867) was even more forceful and antithetical than Augustine on Christ's particular atonement and God's effectual saving desire, occasioning the biggest theological controversy of the ninth century, involving several councils, the leading churchmen of western Europe, and even the successors of Emperor Charlemagne: his son and grandsons. For his stand for the truth, confessor Gottschalk was excommunicated, brutally flogged on two occasions, and placed under house arrest, dying after twenty years in captivity. This recent book contains many excellent writings of Gottschalk never before published in English.

Gumerlock, Francis X. *Fulgentius of Ruspe on the Saving Will of God: The Development of a Sixth-Century African Bishop's Interpretation of I Timothy 2:4 During the Semi-Pelagian Controversy.* Lewiston, NY: Edwin Mellen Press, 2009. In 520, Fulgentius of Ruspe (468–533) wrote a synodal letter, in the name of his fifteen fellow North African bishops (who were banished by the Vandals to Sardinia), opposing the well-meant-offer views of the

---

3   For more, see Angus Stewart, "The *Geneva Theses* (1649): A Recently Uncovered Jewel" *(British Reformed Journal* 62 [Spring/Summer 2015], 27–42), which also cites three other Genevan confessions against an unfulfilled divine wish to save everybody, including Theodore Beza's Confession (1560) and the Formula Consensus Helvetica (1675), produced and promoted by John Henry Heidegger (1633–98) of Zurich, Lucas Gernler (1625–75) of Basel, and Francis Turretin (1623–87) of Geneva (www.cprf.co.uk/articles/genevatheses.html).

semi-Pelagian monks in Constantinople. Gumerlock's fascinating book traces the development of Fulgentius' views through several stages until he confessed the full Augustinian position and embraced the predestinarian understanding of Matthew 23:37, 1 Timothy 2:4, and 2 Peter 3:9.

Knox, John. *On Predestination, in Answer to the Cavillations by an Anabaptist* (1560). In *The Works of John Knox*, edited by David Laing, 5:7–468. Edinburgh: Banner of Truth Trust, 2014. In his longest and most profound theological work, John Knox (c.1514–72) establishes the absolute sovereignty of God from scripture, with frequent appeals to Augustine (including his *Enchiridion*), Calvin (including his *Consensus Genevensis*), and Theodore Beza (1519–1605). When his English Anabaptist opponent argued from the four frequently cited texts (see below) for a desire of God to save the reprobate, Scotland's greatest reformer successfully refuted him on all of them.[4]

Moore, Jonathan. *English Hypothetical Universalism: John Preston and the Softening of Reformed Theology*. Grand Rapids, MI: Eerdmans, 2007. In setting forth the free-offer theology of John Preston (1587–1628) regarding the divine decree, the death of Christ, and the gospel call, Moore explains how it was a watering down of the solid Elizabethan particularism of John Bridges (1536–1618), William Perkins (1558–1602), and John Dove (1561–1618) in Puritan England, as well as being contrary to such continental Reformed worthies as Theodore Beza in Geneva and Jacobus Kimedoncius (c.1550–96) and Jeremias Bastingius (1551–95) in Heidelberg.

Du Moulin, Pierre. *Anatomie of Arminianism*. London: T. S. for Nathaniel Newbery, 1620. Du Moulin (1568–1658) was one

---

4   See "John Knox on the Four Main Texts Cited in Support of a Failed Desire of God to Save Everybody" (www.cprf.co.uk/quotes/knoxsavingdesire.html).

of the four representatives delegated by the French Reformed Church to the great Synod of Dordt (1618–19) but was forbidden to go by King Louis XIII under pain of death. In writing against the doctrines of the Arminians, du Moulin strongly opposed their notion that God wishes to save everyone.[5]

Rainbow, Jonathan. *The Will of God and the Cross: An Historical and Theological Study of John Calvin's Doctrine of Limited Redemption.* Eugene, OR: Pickwick Publications, 1990. In this powerful work, Rainbow convincingly demonstrates that Calvin stands in the line of Augustine of Hippo, Fulgentius of Ruspe, Gottschalk of Orbais, and others, including the Strasbourg reformer Martin Bucer (1491–1551), on Christ's particular atonement and God's saving will toward his elect alone.

The Four Main Texts Wrongly Appealed To as if They Taught the Well-Meant Offer

Besides the authorities from various ages and countries mentioned above (including Augustine, Fulgentius, Gottschalk, Calvin, Knox, Beza, Bridges, Kimedoncius, Bastingius, Perkins, Dove, du Moulin, the Geneva Theses, Turretin, Gernler, Heidegger, Kuyper, Rainbow, Engelsma, and Moore), quotations from and about other theologians, who do not interpret the four main texts urged by free-offer advocates as if they support a (temporal and failed) desire of God to save the reprobate, have been compiled online.[6]

1) 1 Timothy 2:4 includes Januarius, Caesarius of Arles, Students of Cassiodorus (sixth century), an old Irish gloss (c.700),

---

5 For quotes, see "Pierre du Moulin (1568–1658) Against a Universal Divine Saving Desire" (www.cprf.co.uk/quotes/dumoulinsavingdesire.html).

6 For additional online materials (audios, videos, books, articles, and quotes) on this subject, see "Resources on God's Effectual Saving Desire" (www.cprf.co.uk/effectualdesireresources.htm).

Sedulius Scottus, Florus of Lyon, Prudentius of Troyes, Servatus Lupus, Ratramnus of Corbie, Remigius of Lyon, Hugh of St. Victor, Peter Lombard, Bonaventure, Thomas Aquinas, Duns Scotus, Thomas Bradwardine, Gregory of Rimini, John Wycliffe, Laurenzo Valla, Martin Bucer, Jerome Zanchius, Zacharias Ursinus, Daniel Tossanus, William Ames, Jacobus Trigland, Thomas Watson, Herman Witsius, Bernardinus de Moor, Johann van den Honert, Hendrik de Cock, William Cunningham, George Smeaton, Lorraine Boettner, John W. Robbins, Peter Barnes, and more.[7]

Apart from the worthies mentioned in the select bibliography and in connection with 1 Timothy 2:4 (above), the text upon which the free-offer debate has focused historically, quotations from other theologians are also given regarding the three remaining scriptural passages below.

2) Ezekiel 18:23, 32 and 33:11 includes Wilhelmus à Brakel, James Henley Thornwell, John Kennedy of Dingwall, Herman Hoeksema, John H. Gerstner, Richard A. Muller, John Bolt, Christopher J. Connors, Raymond A. Blacketer, Sean Gerety, and more.[8]

3) Matthew 23:37 and Luke 13:34 includes Peter Martyr Vermigli, John Owen, Christopher Ness, Peter Nahuys, John Gill, William Young, Richard Bacon, W. Gary Crampton, James R. Whyte, Matthew Winzer, James Gracie, Vincent Cheung, and more.[9]

4) 2 Peter 3:9 includes the Venerable Bede, the Geneva Bible (1599), the Confession of Tarcal (1562) and Torda (1563), David Dickson, Stephen Charnock, Matthew Henry, Thomas E. Peck, A. W. Pink, Gordon H. Clark, Robert L. Reymond, R. C. Sproul, and more.[10]

---

7 "Quotes on 1 Timothy 2:4" (www.cprf.co.uk/quotes/1timothy2v4.html).

8 "Quotes on Ezekiel 18:23, 32 and 33:11" (www.cprf.co.uk/quotes/ezekiel 33v11.htm).

9 "Quotes on Matthew 23:37 and Luke 13:34" (www.cprf.co.uk/quotes/matthew 23v37.htm).

10 "Quotes on 2 Peter 3:9" (www.cprf.co.uk/quotes/2peter3v9.htm).

Index of Names

A

Academy of Saumur and Saumur theologians...57–58, 65–66, 73, 79, 85, 87–88, 158

Acts of Synod 1924 of the Christian Reformed Church...ix, 176

Acts of Synod 1967 of the Christian Reformed Church...197

Acts of Synod 1980 of the Christian Reformed Church...215

Algra, Hendrik...163

Amyraldism...57–77, 79, 90, 94, 96, 119, 157–59, 217, 229

Amyraut, Moise...34, 57–67, 72–74, 79, 85, 91, 146, 179

Anselm...16

Aquinas, Thomas...72

Arminianism...50, 67–68, 76, 79, 83, 91, 93–94, 102, 106, 113, 130–31, 133, 179, 181, 192, 195, 203–5, 211, 213, 241

Arminians...34, 41–51, 67–72, 80, 91, 103, 107, 124, 131, 146, 189, 213, 215, 222, 225

Arminius, Jacob...70–72, 179

Armstrong, Brian G...60–61, 63

Arrowsmith, John...84–85, 89

Athanasius...2

Auchterarder Creed...97, 99

Auchterarder Presbytery...97

Augustine...xii, 1–4, 6–8, 11–13, 15–16, 70–72, 204, 213

B

Baillie of Amyraut...84, 89

Balcanqual, Walter...80

Baro, Peter...93–94

Bavinck, Herman...5, 43, 169–71, 178

Baxter, Richard...94

Beardslee, John W. III...143–46

Beeke, Joel R...162

Berkhof, Louis...192

Beza, Theodore...57–59

Bogerman, Johannes...80

Bolsec, Jerome...30, 59

Boston, Thomas...98, 100

Bouma, Clarence...167–68

Brakel, Wilhelmus...152–55

Brummelkamp, Anthony...162–63

C

Caesarius of Arles...10–11

Calamy, Edmund...84–85, 89

Calvinists...34–35, 84, 89, 91, 131, 158

Cameron, John...57–60, 85, 88

Candlish, Robert...118, 120

Carleton, Dudley...79–80

Cassian...4–5

Christian Reformed Church...ix, 42, 47, 128–29, 135–36, 166–67, 171–74, 178, 180, 183–84, 186–88, 191–92, 194–95, 197, 199, 203–4, 213, 215

Church of Scotland...97–98, 100, 102, 104, 109–10, 200

Index of Names

INDEX OF SCRIPTURE AND CREEDS